StyleCity
NEW YORK

StyleCity

NEW YORK

With over 350 color photographs and 7 maps

SANDWICH w/ 7.9
PESTO MAYO

HICKEN SALA

IOLI w/ MARINARA

OLIVE TAPENA

Contents

Street Wise

Style Traveler

Series concept and editor: Lucas Dietrich
Research and author: Alice Twemlow
Original design and map concept: The Senate
Jacket and book design: Grade Design Consultants
Maps: Peter Bull

Specially commissioned photography by
Ingrid Rasmussen and Anthony Webb

Although every effort has been made to ensure that
the information in this book is as up-to-date and as
accurate as possible at the time of going to press,
some details are liable to change.

First published in the United Kingdom in 2003 by
Thames & Hudson Ltd, 181A High Holborn, London
WC1V 7QX

www.thamesandhudson.com

British Library Cataloguing-in-Publication Data
A catalogue record for this book is available from the
British Library

ISBN 0-500-21007-1

Printed in China

How to Use This Guide

The book features two principal sections: **Street Wise** and **Style Traveler**.

Street Wise, which is arranged by neighborhood, features areas that can be covered in a day (and night) on foot and includes a variety of locations – cafés, shops, restaurants, museums, performance spaces, bars – that capture local flavor or are lesser-known destinations.

The establishments in the **Style Traveler** section represent the city's best and most characteristic locations – 'worth a detour' – and feature hotels (**sleep**), restaurants (**eat**), cafés and bars (**drink**), boutiques and shops (**shop**) and getaways (**retreat**).

Each location is shown as a circled number on the relevant neighborhood map, which is intended to provide a rough idea of location and proximity to major sights and landmarks rather than precise position. Locations in each neighborhood are presented sequentially by map number. Each entry in the **Style Traveler** has two numbers: the top one refers to the page number of the neighborhood map on which it appears; the second number is its location.

For example, the visitor might begin by selecting a hotel from the **Style Traveler** section. Upon arrival, **Street Wise** might lead him to the best joint for coffee before guiding him to a house-museum nearby. After lunch he might go to find a special jewelry store listed in the **shop** section. For a memorable dining experience, he might consult his neighborhood section to find the nearest restaurant crossreferenced to **eat** in **Style Traveler**.

Street addresses are given in each entry, and complete information – including email and web addresses – is listed in the alphabetical **contact** section. Travel and contact details for the destinations in **retreat** are given at the end of **contact**.

Legend

- (2)   Location
-    Museums, sights
-    Gardens, squares
- (S)   Subway stops
-    Streets

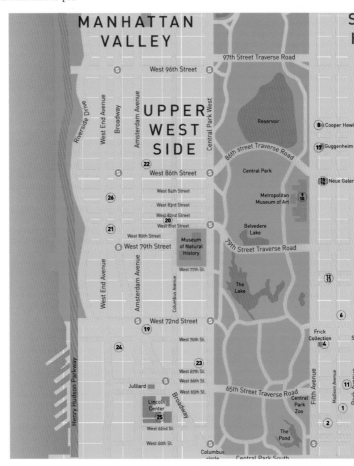

NEW YORK

To Walt Whitman in "City of Ships," New York was a "Proud and passionate city! Mettlesome, mad, extravagant city!" The refrain of E. B. White's poignant 1949 essay "Here is New York" is "the essential fever of New York." Architect Rem Koolhaas's 1978 socio-architectural analysis of New York is titled *Delirious New York*, and it's not just a conceit. The recurring reference to mania in the various literary, musical and artistic responses to the city throughout its history is hardly surprising: New York is as much a sensibility as it is a topographically defined area. Temperatures, temperaments, expectations and spectacles are exaggerated in this densely packed can of about eight million sardines. The biggest bagels, the fastest taxi cabs, the biggest economic disparity, the skinniest lattes — it's truly a city of superlatives.

Unlike most other contemporary metropolises, Manhattan cannot sprawl and become a conurbation. Two rivers confine its expansion to the vertical axis. It can move upwards and it can transplant attitudinal seedlings to the outer boroughs, but growth mainly occurs in a folding fashion, in and on top of itself. The friction generated by this "culture of congestion," as Koolhaas dubbed it, is both New York's virtue and its vice. Creation and destruction go hand in hand in a city that is in a constant state of renewal. Just as in 1947, when the architect Le Corbusier wrote, "New York is not a completed city, it is a city in the process of becoming," today's city continues to demolish and build itself, expanding into and reinventing new neighborhoods, discarding others at dizzying velocity. The most visible of the construction sites is an area of Lower Manhattan, popularly known as Ground Zero, which is currently being shaped to Polish-born and Bronx-bred architect Daniel Libeskind's 1776-foot-tall (840-metre) vision.

Catalyzing this creative cauldron are the combined visions of restaurateurs, club promoters, designers, boutique curators and gallerists who are constantly pushing at the boundaries of neighborhoods and their lifestyle culture. In a given neighborhood's renewal it is the period of transition when feverish renovation grinds against day-to-day life of the area's inhabitants that is the most fascinating and highly charged. The "completeness" of a locale's transformation is always its death knell. Luc Sante has characterized New York as a city where "the navel of the world and the frontier of civilization lie a few blocks apart. And therein lies its energy."

While the surface of the city is continually undergoing cosmetic surgery – a global-brand store tuck here and an injection of Botox to banish the drug addicts there – the substructure of old and fantastical Gotham is never far away. Steam wheezes out of manholes, a reminder of the city's ancient heating system. You can glimpse traces of painted advertising signage on the walls of buildings. In the summer children play in the jets of water hydrants as if in a 1930s Weegee photograph, and subway air-vents near the Flatiron building still send skirts flying.

New York, and specifically Manhattan, is a walking city. At 13.5 by 2.5 miles wide (at 14th Street; 21.5 by 4 kilometers), it is possible to traverse much of Manhattan's length and breadth in a day. There are many ways of walking ranging from the corporate executive's streamlined march to the self-evolved wide-legged shuffle of Lower East Side kids, whose movements are restricted by the need to prevent their low-slung pants from falling off. On the whole, the walking is of a speed unmatched by other cities. This pace, just like the reasoning behind the '212' dialling code for Manhattan – the numerals are the closest together on the telephone dial pad, making it the speediest code to dial – are necessitated by the brevity of the New York minute.

At the risk of annoying native street-walkers, as a first-time or repeat visitor to the city you might try a particularly fine mode of transport originally expounded by Situationist Guy Debord in 1958: "drifting," or "a technique of rapid passage through varied ambiences" is still a superior way in which to absorb a city's "psychogeographical contours." As you walk, allow yourself to be free of life's ordinary motivations. Be drawn by your instinct, send your gaze upward, allow yourself to overhear conversations – whether its the loud-mouthed, wisecracking exchange between deli-server and customer or an aesthetic difference in opinion between a lady-who-lunches and her personal shopper in Bergdorf Goodman.

This book offers ideas for staging posts along the paths of your forays. In the following pages you will find exceptional designed environments and experiences that are idiosyncratic to New York and stylish in unconventional ways. They range from classic 19th-century spit-and-sawdust saloons, Jewish delicatessens and gas-lit chophouses that have withstood the churn of constant urban renewal, to the sleek lounges, chic cafés, exquisitely assembled boutiques and utterly contemporary hotels that are heralded as bastions of cool. If there is a unifying gesture in the eclectic spectrum of New York's most exuberant play-spaces and refined oases for repose, then it is panache. Extreme panache.

Street Wise

We were here before you were Born.

McSorley's

TriBeCa • Chinatown • Little Italy • NoLIta • SoHo • NoHo • Chelsea • Meatpacking District • West Village • Gramercy Park • East Village • Lower East Side • Lower Manhattan • Midtown • Upper East Side • Upper West Side • Harlem • Williamsburg • Long Island City • Park Slope • Smith Street • Fort Greene

TriBeCa

Chinatown

Little Italy

NoLIta

SoHo

NoHo

New York is a city of transitioning neighborhoods and nowhere is their ebb and flow more apparent than in the acronym-happy villages below and around Houston Street. The once-decaying industrial area now known as TriBeCa (Triangle Below Canal) began to be converted into residential lofts in the late 1970s by artists deserting SoHo because of rising rents. Over the following two decades, A-listers – Robert De Niro among them – snapped up gargantuan lofts in late-19th-century cast-iron buildings and the area's population increased exponentially. Chic eateries soon followed, and today the area is completely gentrified, with a host of furniture and architectural salvage stores and a sprinkling of fashion boutiques.

The sudden shift from one community to the next within the space of a block is continually startling. One minute you are walking in a sea of red plastic bags, the unofficial logos of Chinatown's food markets, and the next you are hit by the smell of salami and coffee wafting out of one of the remaining Italian fine-food stores. There are few places in Little Italy that still give a sense of its storied past: the Ravenite Social Club on Mulberry Street, for example, which was celebrity don John Gotti's headquarters from the mid-1980s until his arrest in 1990, is now a handbag and accessories store. But there are some that still give you a whiff, albeit a friendlier one, of what it used to be like on these mean streets. The district known as NoLIta (North of Little Italy) is the area with the highest concentration of new boutiques and Europhile cafés. These businesses sprang up in the late 1990s and, in a heartbeat, displaced a Sicilian community. The term NoLIta describes a fashionable lifestyle as much as it does a geographical area.

SoHo was the center of New York's art scene from the 1970s until the mid-1990s when chain stores started to move in, raising the rents, ousting old stalwarts and pushing its interesting stores and galleries to areas outside its perimeter. Although SoHo's heyday has long passed, the beauty of the area's distinctive cast-iron buildings with their zigzag fire escapes, the bottle-glass sidewalks that allow light into storage vaults below, streets of Belgian brick and traces of Jean-Michel Basquiat's graffiti heritage here and there can cause you to forget for a second the rude invasion of global brands.

Hiding to the east of the strip-mall of lower Broadway and continuing north of Houston Street is a little-spoilt oasis called NoHo, with Bond Street as its primary spokes-street. The ground floors of 19th-century loft buildings with façades of marble, cast iron, limestone and terracotta are largely returned to their original usage as retail stores.

CONTEMPORARY DESIGN
2 **Totem**
71 Franklin Street

This design store is part of an empire that includes a sister gallery space in SoHo – designed by the ubiquitous Karim Rashid – a magazine and an online TV channel. With regularly mobbed parties, it is a major player in New York's contemporary design scene. Totem represents 30 or so well-known designers and manufacturers from Europe and the United States. The exhibitions tend to be nationally themed, recent examples including Icelandic, Canadian and Japanese showcases. David Shearer, its founder, was inspired by a conversation he had with Ray Eames about the "totems" that she and her husband had garnered from their travels and that influenced their work.

VAULTED GASTRONOMY
3 **Bouley**
120 West Broadway

Twelve-foot (4-meter) half-moon windows, low Guastavino-style vaulted ceilings hung with chandeliers and walls painted blood red provide a suitably dramatic setting for chef David Bouley's culinary spectacles. The five-course tasting menu includes an appetizer called "Return from Chiang Mai" that features chilled Maine lobster, mango, fresh artichoke, Serrano ham and passion fruit, fresh coconut and Kaffir lime dressing.

URBAN IDYLL
4 **Duane Park**
Intersection of Duane and Hudson Streets

Nestled in the middle of a busy intersection in TriBeCa is an unexpected green triangle of calm and beauty. New York's second oldest public park has the active support of locals, who look after its historical importance and keep it fresh with new plantings. Lying at the heart of TriBeCa, it also provides a good vantage point from which to observe the richly detailed brick buildings that surround it.

BRIGHT LIGHTS, BIG CITY
5 **Odeon**

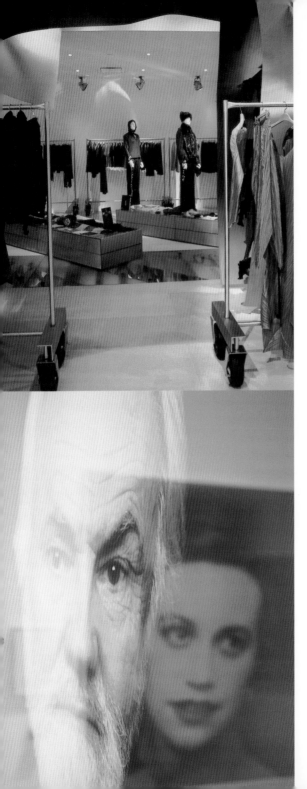

SCULPTING FASHION

7 TriBeCa Issey Miyake
119 Hudson Street

This store, on the ground floor of a TriBeCa cast-iron building, carries Miyake's women's and men's lines, including his experimental A-POC clothing, and all the accessories and fragrances. Frank Gehry collaborated with the architecture firm G Tects to create the titanium tsunami wave that dominates the store's interior. Many of the techniques used for the Bilbao Guggenheim were applied to create the billows and curves of the metallic structure that offsets the Japanese designer's convention-busting wares.

NOUVELLE COMFORT FOOD

8 Théo
325 Spring Street

A "modern American bistro" with a lounge upstairs is the latest refined offering from multi-tasking restaurant, bar and hotel entrepreneur Jonathan Morr. Sited in a former 1940s United Parcel Service building, with industrial fishbowl windows, it has an interior designed in glossy black wood, glass tile and cream, by Frederique Gormand, a former employee of Christian Liaigre of Mercer Hotel fame. The menu errs in favor of nouvelle comfort food – macaroni and fontina cheese ravioli and fish 'n' chips, for instance – and a range of appetizers such as minted eggplant spread on flatbread are intended for sharing.

HANGAR-SIZED ART SPACE

9 Ace Gallery
275 Hudson Street

This enormous white-walled warehouse space – and although far west of the gallery circuits of Chelsea and SoHo, it's worth the walk – stages infrequent large and complex installations by artists such as Issey Miyake, Richard Serra and Tim Hawkinson. For a recent laser art show by the Japanese artist Hiro Yamagata, 30 technicians were required to install in the 25,000-square-foot (2,300-square-meter) gallery a grid of holographic Mylar panels and hang motorized, mirrored cubes that spun at programed intervals to refract high-tech laser and fiber-optic beams.

DEPARTMENT STORE, CHINESE STYLE

10 Pearl River Mart

477 Broadway

Household wares that span the spectrum from exotic chic to practical necessity are crazily crammed into the two floors of this Chinese department store. Join a melee of Chinese grannies buying electric rice cookers and hip young women finding accessories for their NoLIta boutiques. Jostle for t'ai chi slippers, beaded flip-flops and dragon-embroidered jackets, paper goods and brilliantly decorated porcelain tea mugs.

STREET ARCHITECTURE

11 Storefront for Art and Architecture

97 Kenmare Street

Designed by Steven Holl and Vito Acconci in 1993, this gallery space for architectural thought and practice bursts beyond its tiny slice-of-pie footprint. The irregularly rectilinear plates in the concrete-board façade revolve on vertical and horizontal pivots so they can flip open to the street, making the space an exercise in mutable architecture.

PEOPLE-WATCHING AND COFFEE

12 Caffé Roma

154

GODFATHERS' SOCIAL CLUB

13 Mare Chiaro

158

UNDERGROUND SCENE

14 Double Happiness

173 Mott Street

In former incarnations, Double Happiness was a speakeasy, a shady Italian restaurant and a mob-run gay bar. Today, the basement bar, along with the newly opened Happy Ending, on nearby Broome Street, is the scenic backdrop for a bevy of beautiful people bopping to the strains of regular DJs as they sip on their green-tea Martini house specials. The interior incorporates a giant abacus as a window between two sections of the bar and there is a variety of seating options beneath the open brickwork arches.

DESTINATION CHINESE CLASSICS

15 Peking Duck House

28 Mott Street

The interior is unusually minimal for a Chinese restaurant. But once you are served your platters of delicately crisp duck skin with stacks of house-made pancakes, and green scallions, fresh cucumbers and special hoisin sauce, you won't be looking up again to notice. The bring-your-own wine policy and reasonably priced food mean that a large group can eat handsomely for less than $15 a head.

CELLULOID COCKTAILS

16 Screening Room

157

THE BOHEMIAN VIBE

17 Knitting Factory

74 Leonard Street

New York's downtown experimental music establishment is a honeycomb of rooms and bars on four floors that on any one night might be hosting an alternative film festival, jazz in the Tap Room, hip-hop poetry readings or performances by the likes of John Lury, Sonic Youth or Carl Craig. The main performance space, with an intimate capacity of only 250, is a great place to see up-and-coming bands in a seriously bohemian setting.

HOTEL BAR REDEFINED

18 Church Lounge

Tribeca Grand Hotel, 2 Sixth Avenue

Instead of a restaurant, the TriBeCa Grand offers casual dining in the various plush seating areas scattered throughout its large atrium. In the evening, the left side of the triangular bar, especially the semi-private Chambers Lounge, becomes a hot spot. The DJ program is consistently good – spin guests include the Eighteenth Street Lounge heavyweights Thunderball and Blue States – and some of the most glamorous parties are held here – Fischerspooner's after-show party recently filled the lounge with leg-warmer-wearing Electroclash groupies.

LOBBYING POWER

19 Tribeca Grand Hotel

132

Bounded by the Bowery to the east, Lafayette to the west, Houston to the north and overlapping with Little Italy to the south is the province known as NoLIta. Mott, Mulberry and Elizabeth Streets, in particular, are lined with meticulously curated boutiques that open and close like so many pretty butterflies. Albanese Meats and Poultry, sitting resiliently in a street now recast by trend-setting young retailers, is an original relic from a time when the area was a Sicilian enclave.

If you can get (and keep) a table at this buzzing corner luncheonette, use it as your NoLIta model-watching HQ. The nuevo-Mexican/Cuban menu offers a range of spicy dishes, but the grilled corncob rolled in grated cotija cheese and chilli powder and sprinkled with lime juice is the one the regulars go for.

Hand-painted, banana-leaf wallpaper lines the walls (you can buy rolls of it at the desk), the music is just right, and there is a stylish range of casual T-shirts, anoraks and trousers in this tasty morsel of a menswear boutique.

This corner bistro is not yet as overrun with gazelles toting Calypso shopping bags as its neighbors Gitane and Habana. The interior evokes a Viennese café, with its black-and-white-tiled floor and Eastern European-tinged menu. Café Lebowitz, the latest contribution from Brian McNally and his brother Pete, is apparently named after humorist Fran Lebowitz. The cafe is most neighborly in the afternoon when you can enjoy a coffee and strudel and watch the young NoLIta entrepreneurs pacing their estate.

Brazilian owners, Lipe Midieres and Ana Abdul, have mixed lifestyle shoppers a readymade cocktail of books, house wares and clothing at this intriguing store. International labels include Stella McCartney, Lucien Pellat-Finet and Tufi Duek. Great finds to be had among the eclectic stock include Courrèges bags.

INA is the civilized choice for designer consignment shopping. In an atmosphere that is far more refined than the meltdown-inducing Century 21, you'll find an array of discerningly picked designer clothes, accessories and shoes in pristine condition – some are samples. INA's self-described purpose is to "select only what's in fashion from those who are in fashion for those who want to be in fashion." Join other NoLIta girls and boys who spent too much on their brunch for a rummage through the racks that burst with wares from the likes of Helmut Lang, Prada, Vivienne Westwood and Kors.

This small gallery puts on curated shows and reflects the inspirations and process behind the irregularly appearing and limited-edition *Visionaire* album. Conceived by Stephan Gan, Cecilia Dean and James Kaliardos, the couture version of a regular magazine has taken various forms and involved luminaries from the worlds of fashion, art and design. A recent issue, titled *Love*, was created from 4,000 hardcover novels, hand-assembled with inserts from fashion designers, models, writers, illustrators – Björk, Matthew Barney, Nick Knight, Mario Testino, Philip Treacy and Jonathan Safran Foer, to name a few – and finished with a sterling-silver heart on a black silk cord by legendary jewelry designer Elsa Peretti for Tiffany & Co.

THE SOHO BRASSERIE EPITOMIZED

36 Balthazar

80 Spring Street

Even if you don't have time for a multistory iced-shellfish platter at this infamous SoHo brasserie, make sure you do, at the very least, breeze in and out, either to pick up a croissant in the adjoining pint-sized patisserie or for a bowl of steaming café au lait in the bar area. Worn red leather banquettes, age-spotted mirrors and nicotine-stained paint were used to create an already aged French bistro look in this airy 180-table space. "I didn't have in mind a particular restaurant in France that I was trying to imitate," says owner Keith McNally, "but there are bits and experiences of various restaurants that have stuck with me." Balthazar is one of those contemporary SoHo landmarks – others include the Prada store, Dean and Deluca, the window of Pleats Please, the bathroom at Bar 89 – that you just have to see; they are part of the deal.

SUBLIME HANDCRAFTED JEWELRY

37 Ted Muehling

27 Howard Street

Pay homage to craftsmanship and beauty at this minimal store dissembling as a gallery space. Muehling's sculptural jewelry is inspired by organic forms such as shells, rocks, coral, eggs and berries. The pared-down shapes are exquisitely rendered in brushed gold or finely hammered metal. His delicate ceramic work is manufactured at the Nymphenburg porcelain factory in Germany. Muehling's work along with decorative objects by Gabriella Kiss, Lee Hale, and Stephan Allendorf is displayed simply in tall glass cases.

BATHROOM LIGHTS FANTASTIC

38 Bar 89

89 Mercer Street

If you need to use a bathroom, make a beeline for Bar 89. The high-ceilinged main space uses glass and steel for a somewhat self-conscious minimalist effect. While the cocktails are large and powerful and the menu of bar snacks appealing, it is the bathroom on the balcony that gives cause for real delight. The doors to the unisex stalls are seemingly transparent until you close the latch and the glass becomes opaque.

CURATORIAL EXPERIMENTATION

39 Artists Space

38 Greene Street, 3rd Floor

A pioneer in the alternative-space movement, Artists Space was founded in 1972 as a non-profit institution supporting contemporary artists. Today the gallery is one of the few exhibition spaces to exploit the dynamic interchange between practice that involves design, video, performance, architecture and art. A recent exhibition titled "Infotecture" examined how information is handled by designers and architects and featured the projects of Foundation 33, Diller + Scofidio and the Bureau of Inverse Technology, among others. In its 25-year history, Artists Space has presented the work of over 5,000 emerging artists.

BALTHAZAR

CAFÉ

SPÉCIALITÉS DE VINS

40 Donald Judd House
101 Spring Street

This five-story building on the northeast corner of Spring and Mercer Streets was purchased in 1968 by the Archdeacon of Minimalism, furniture maker and artist, Donald Judd. The 1870 cast-iron building is now managed by Judd's estate. You can look through the ground-floor windows and see some of Judd's pieces, as well as the work of Carl Andre and Dan Flavin, two of the artists whose work he collected. While the inaccessibility of the building's interior may be frustrating, it's a lot easier than traveling to Marfa, Texas, the town that Judd has transformed into an art installation.

41 Supreme
274 Lafayette Street

Follow the skateboarders to this fresh little store that stocks T-shirts, sweats and shoes from Goodenough, DC shoes, Analog, Burton, Gravis, Girl, Chocolate, as well as the store's own label. The video wall, Futura artwork and display of decks – including Supreme's own PMS paint-chip design – is its own art gallery. For more skate togs on the same street, try Triple Five Soul (no. 290) or X-Large (no. 265).

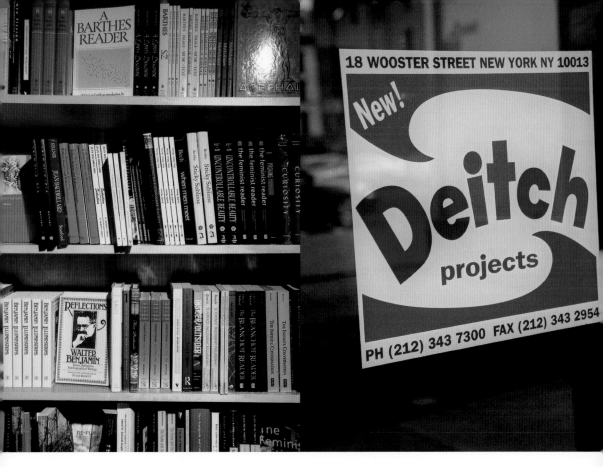

The New Museum is a smartly curated, three-level space in the middle of SoHo. Its program of shows examines key moments in the development of contemporary art and new media within their social and cultural contexts. Some recent exhibitions include "Super-ficial: The Surfaces of Architecture in a Digital Age" and "Living Inside the Grid." The bookstore on the basement floor stocks an excellent selection of art and design volumes, including monographs, exhibition catalogs and periodicals, as well as multiples and limited-edition artworks by artists such as Rob Pruitt, Christian Boltanski, William Kentridge, Bruce Nauman and Andres Serrano.

Some of the most ambitious presentations of emerging art, design and music take place in Jeffrey Deitch's two SoHo project spaces. With an A-list of international artists and friends at Deitch's beck and call – Vanessa Beecroft, Fischerspooner, Chris Johanson, Barry McGee, Mariko Mori and 1980s legend Keith Haring among them – the experimental gallery owner is able to assemble shows that enchant even the most jaded of New York's "artgentsia." The Wooster space, the size of a garage, hosts occasional site-specific installations and performances – a recent show, "Session the Bowl," featured a kidney-shaped skating bowl, replete with skaters, by the artist collective Simparch. The more intimate Grand Street gallery is home to a regular program of exhibits.

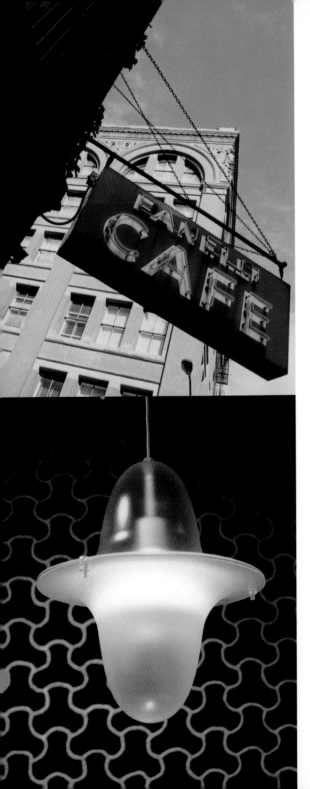

If you feel that your hotel room distances you from the way your contemporaries live in this city, then take a trip to The Apartment, a store designed to make you feel right at home – albeit a rather idealized home. The owners, Gina Alverez and Stefan Boublil, have divided the two-floor space into areas that represent a living room, office, bedroom, kitchen, bathroom and closet. Didier Chaudanson's snap-together lights, Freecell's tractor chairs and Kenyan Lewis's fly riding caps can all be found in the appropriate room, and sometimes you can pick up coffee and snacks in the kitchen.

Fanelli's has been serving food and drink in inimitable, no-nonsense style since 1847. This genuine bar, incongruous in its central SoHo location, has managed to weather a fashion tempest that has swept along Prince Street, leaving bland chain stores in its desultory wake. Bob the bartender is a retired prizefighter and a wall of original boxing photographs and portraits from the early 1900s pay tribute to the pugilist's art.

With a colorful "Vacation" in your hand (the bar's signature drink, available in pink, green or blue), you are ready to lounge on a brocaded ottoman or the long cowhide couch in this classic SoHo watering hole. The fabulousness of the rustic but comfortable mountain lodge-style bar is nicely faded like a pair of well-worn jeans. John McDonald, the restaurateur, owns both the Merc Bar and the Marc Newson-designed subterranean Canteen right around the corner. He is also the editor and publisher of the fairly new design, fashion and food rag, *City NY*, a stylish magazine McDonald sees as the American take on *Wallpaper**.

MOM-AND-POP SHOP

48 Vesuvio Bakery Shop
160 Prince Street

You may well recognize this tiny Depression-era bakery from its countless appearances in advertisements and films, including *The Prince of Tides*. Anthony Dapolito, a local character and key figure in SoHo politics, continues the family running of the business. Its gold-stencilled window still displays homemade Italian bread and tarellas (pepper biscuits) in spite of the enforced evacuation of nearly all of SoHo's other mom-and-pop shops.

HALF-MILE OF BRASS RODS

49 Broken Kilometer
393 West Broadway

Viewing land artist Walter de Maria's installation of 500 highly polished, solid brass rods precisely placed in five parallel rows is a strangely ethereal experience.

FRAGRANCE LABORATORY

50 Helmut Lang Perfumerie
81 Greene Street

Gluckman Mayner Architects' store for Helmut Lang provides a suitably hard-edged laboratory setting for the minimal designer's fragrance line. The narrow entry is emphasized by an LED installation by Jenny Holzer that runs the length of the interior along the top of an enameled steel wall.

FASHION SUPERMARKET

51 Kirna Zabete

NATURAL SANCTUARY

52 The New York Earth Room
141 Wooster Street

Created in 1977 by American artist Walter de Maria, this pastoral sculpture consists of one SoHo loft and 250 cubic yards (190 cubic meters) of dark topsoil, weighing 280,000 pounds (127,000 kg).

STATE OF THE ART

53 Apple Store
103 Prince Street

Need to check your e-mail? Avoid the charges at passé cybercafés and pop into the Apple Store, where you can log on at one of Apple's latest computers. Aside from the array of state-of-the-art digital cameras, iPods and Mac accessories in this gleaming white space designed by Bohlin Cywinski Jackson and Ronette Riley, there is a so-called "Genius Bar" for getting your technical questions answered and an amphitheatre where workshops and demonstrations are held.

DESIGN MUSEUM

54 Moss

JAPANESE SOBA RESTAURANT

55 Honmura An
170 Mercer Street

This Japanese restaurant is renowned for the quality of its soba noodles. They are made on the premises from locally bought buckwheat and presented in handsome lacquer boxes, accompanied by various dipping sauces. In a famous *New York Times* review, restaurant critic Ruth Reichl gave the restaurant three stars, a rating previously unheard-of for an "ethnic eatery." The serene walk-up SoHo loft space, which features such Zen touches as floating pools of flowers and ceiling-high displays of twisted branches, was designed by the architectural firm Yui and Bloch Design.

LATE-NIGHT SECRET

56 Submercer
Below Mercer Hotel, 147 Mercer Street

One floor below the Mercer Kitchen restaurant in the basement of the still-gorgeous Mercer Hotel is a mini-nightclub with a collective ego out of proportion to its 35-person capacity. Most of the fun is had in finding it. Go through an unmarked exit door off the restaurant, down a flight of steps and along a narrow walkway leading to a smaller, casbah version of the restaurant space, with red lights and intimate nooks.

LOUIS SULLIVAN IN NEW YORK

57 Bayard Building

65 Bleecker Street

The only building in New York designed by American master architect Louis Sullivan, the 15-story bright-white edifice is best viewed from the corner of Houston and Crosby Streets. The way in which the terracotta curtain walls are used to express the building's structural steel frame is a classic example of the style he greatly influenced, the Chicago School.

VERDANT OASIS

58 Liz Christy Garden

Northeast corner of Houston Street and Bowery

Thanks to the work of activist Liz Christy, the Green Guerillas and a 30-strong team of volunteers, NoHo's visitors and residents have a surprisingly ample oasis of oxygen emanating from the northeastern bank of Houston Street. The Liz Christy Garden, founded in 1973 as the first community garden in New York, has a pond with fish and red-eared slider turtles, a beehive and a wildflower habitat, a grape arbor, a grove of weeping birch trees and hundreds of varieties of flowering perennials.

EIGHTIES GLAM SCENE

59 B-Bar

DOMESTIC HISTORY PRESERVED

60 Merchant's House Museum

29 East 4th Street

This 1832 row house is among the finest surviving examples of late-Federal and Greek Revival architecture of the period. The city's only preserved 19th-century home – the residence of the prosperous merchant Seabury Tredwell and his large family – is situated in what was then a fashionable "uptown" district of the city. Three floors of this fascinating home are available for viewing. And, if asked, the knowledgeable docents will explain the details of the formal parlors that feature identical black-and-gold marble mantelpieces, a stunning Ionic double-column screen and mahogany pocket doors separating the rooms. And don't forget the back garden, an otherworldly retreat, restored to 19th-century specifications.

ACCESSORY PALACE

61 Bond 07

CHIC SUSHI

62 Bond Street

WILD-AT-HEART PERFORMANCES

63 Joe's Pub

425 Lafayette Street

Joe's Pub is the wilder sibling of the Joseph Papp Public Theater (look out for Pentagram partner Paula Scher's bold typographic banners on the exterior of the latter). This contemporary take on the cabaret lounge serves up avant-garde music such as a rock opera featuring singers from They Might Be Giants and Hedwig and theatrical performances such as a Shakespearean evening with Steven Berkoff. The nightly after-hours DJ parties are for a crowd of hipsters, often of ambiguous sexuality and resplendent with inconceivable haircuts.

DJ'S DELIGHT

64 Other Music

15 East 4th Street

Manhattan's hands-down best record store, with stock of unclassifiable musical genres, unconventionally categorized as In, Out, Electronica, La Decadanse, Krautrock, Groove, Psychedelia and Then. Most of the hottest gig tickets can be purchased here, and look out for in-store performances from the likes of DJ Shadow, Yo La Tengo, Jim O'Rourke, Tindersticks and Mouse On Mars.

CHURCH OF VODKA

65 Temple Bar

Chelsea
Meatpacking District
West Village

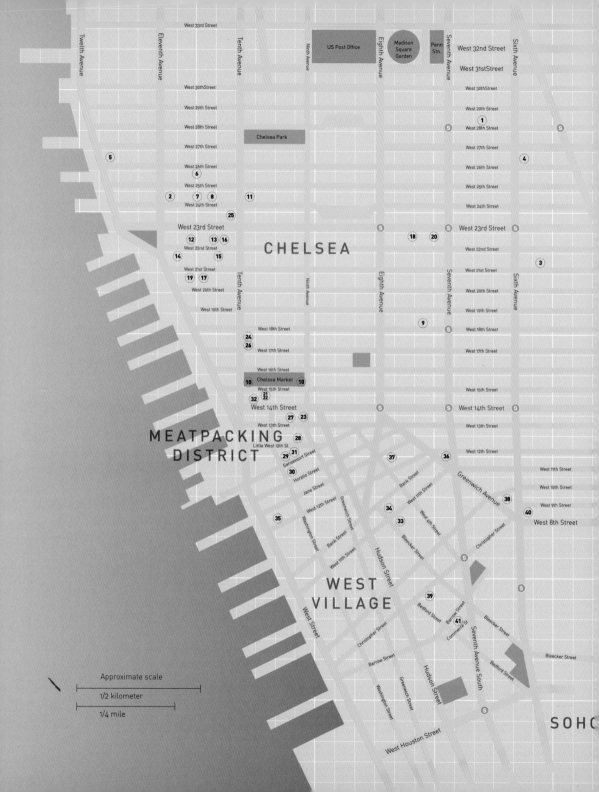

Chelsea takes its name from the estate of Captain Thomas Clarke who, in 1750, retired to the then-rural area after winning glory in the French and Indian Wars. He named the estate for the hospital for retired soldiers in London. By the 1850s Clarke's grandson had developed the area into a proto-suburb of elegant brownstones on tree-lined streets. When landfill was used to extend the waterfront by three avenues, the newly claimed land was taken over by piers, garages and warehouses and tenements to house immigrant workers. And thus a division between eastern residential Chelsea and western industrial Chelsea arose. Apart from the addition of huge apartment buildings such as the 1,670-unit London Terrace in 1930 and public housing projects in the 1960s, there are many blocks in the eastern swath of Chelsea that are little changed since Victorian times. The industrial section, however, has undergone an enormous revitalization since a caravan of blue-chip art galleries began to arrive from SoHo in the mid-1990s. Today's Chelsea has the highest concentration of contemporary art galleries in the world in the "white cube" area enclosed by Tenth and Eleventh Avenues and 20th and 26th Streets, as well as fine examples of converted-use buildings such as the Chelsea Market in an old Nabisco factory. Chelsea's vibrant gay community is reflected in the character of many of the restaurants, clubs and stores that stay open late into the night.

To the south and west of Chelsea is the Meatpacking District, a wholesale meat market since the 1930s. Until the late 1990s, when the designer boutiques, start-ups and restaurants began to invade its lockers, its cobbled streets were the daytime hangout for brawny meat packers and the nighttime catwalks of transsexual prostitutes. Today there are fewer than 30 meat dealers operating in the area and one gets the feeling that they will disappear altogether in the next few years.

Continue your wanderings south through the off-grid streets of the West Village, which, with its low Federal and Greek-revival row houses, plentiful parks and specialist stores, truly feels like a village. Greenwich Village, once the stomping ground of rebellious artists, bohemians and intellectuals, and later the seedbed of numerous contemporary social movements such as feminism and gay liberation, is now a commercialized tourist trap. Stick to its western reaches – the narrow streets that criss-cross Hudson Street and Bleecker – for your explorations.

Development of the riverside beyond the West Side Highway has led to the conversion of the decaying piers – which until recently were used by late-night cruisers – into verdant leisure parks, and a pathway now runs the western length of southern Manhattan, to the delight of cyclists, roller-bladers and joggers.

1 Flower District

West 28th Street, between Sixth and Seventh Avenues

You can catch the scent of this stretch of 28th Street between Sixth and Seventh Avenues well before you reach it. Ever since the 1870s – when flowers became popular for display in upper-class residences – this area has been home to New York's plant and floral wholesalers. Today it is the smallest and most threatened of the City's few remaining single-trade districts. The vendors, specializing in orchids, silk flowers, topiary trees or florists' supplies, use the sidewalks as an extension of their display space so that they become a patchwork of huge crates of variegated tulips and planters of wheatgrass. Even if you don't have time to enter the tiny stores and jostle with party planners and floral designers, merely walking down the street between the hours of 4:30 a.m. and noon is an olfactory and visual experience that should not be missed.

MONUMENTAL WORKS

2 Gagosian Gallery

555 West 24th Street

Heavyweight dealer Larry Gagosian consummated the art world's newfound love for Chelsea when, in 2000, he moved his gallery from SoHo to West 24th Street. With 20,000 square feet (1,860 square meters) of industrial space to play in, Gagosian's is the largest commercial art gallery in Chelsea. One of the first shows to exploit the monumental proportions of the Gluckman Mayner-designed space was Richard Serra's *Torqued Ellipses*. Such 1980s stars as David Salle and Larry Poons show here, as well as several young British artists, including Damien Hirst, Jenny Saville, and the Chapman brothers.

OP-ART CLUB

3 Centro Fly

45 West 21st Street

Named after a Milan department store designed by Gae Aulenti in 1965 and inspired by Victor Vasarely, Centro Fly is a nocturnal palace of mod. Black-and-white Op Art supergraphics, spinning disco balls set in recessed mirrored arches, white leather banquettes, shag-carpeted sunken lounges all amplify the disco theme created by designer and co-owner Sally Bennett. Junior Sanchez is a regular in the DJ booth and is joined by a stream of electronic beat purveyors. The main room holds a crowd of about a thousand people, depending on the energy level of the dance moves.

4 Annex Antiques Fair and Flea Market
Sixth Avenue between 24th and 26th Streets

For an intriguing archaeological dig into Americana's substrata – with furniture, vintage clothing, vintage jewelry, paintings and quirky antiques particularly well represented – look no further than this collection of weekend flea and antiques markets, centered around 26th Street and Sixth Avenue. Come at sunrise for the choice goods and at dusk for the bargains. Hot-dog vendors hover in the vicinity, but a more pleasant refreshment break can be found at the Antique Café at 101 West 25th Street (between Sixth and Seventh Avenues).

MODERNE CREATIVE CENTER
5 Starrett Lehigh Building
601 West 26th Street

This colossal industrial building was built in 1931 by Russell G. & Walter M. Cory and Yasuo Matsui. It might almost be an Art Moderne streamlined ocean liner grounded on the bank of the Hudson River. Its brick spandrels and continuous wraparound windows elicit vistas up and down the Hudson and make this a modernist landmark well worth the trek out west. A few years ago the building saw an influx, followed by a rapid outflux, of dot-commers. Among the current inhabitants are Martha Stewart's studio, the late Jay Chiat's Screaming Media and several noteworthy art galleries and a rare bookstore. An elevator, originally used to hoist freight-train cars and now used by FedEx trucks, can be found at the building's core.

DESIGN WORKS
6 Henry Urbach Architecture
526 West 26th Street

An architect by training, Urbach aims with his gallery to create "a laboratory for investigations into the nature and potential of contemporary space." The investigations have resulted in exhibits of Richard Barnes's photographs of Ted Kaczynski's cabin and the dream-state renderings of experimental architect Lebbeus Woods. Among the experimental architectural studios that Urbach represents are Diller + Scofidio and LOT/EK, who designed the space.

ART DISTRICT PIONEER
7 Matthew Marks Gallery
523 West 24th Street

Marks was the Chelsea art district's primary pioneer. In 1994 he moved his gallery from an apartment space on Madison Avenue to an ambulance garage on a windswept and, apart from the cab drivers washing their cars, deserted 22nd Street. Now he shares with Barbara Gladstone a disused knife factory on 24th Street and his artists include Nan Goldin, Gary Hume, Fischli/Weiss, Roni Horn and Andreas Gursky.

MINIMAL GALLERY
8 Luhring Augustine
531 West 24th Street

This minimal gallery – another Gluckman design – was founded in 1985 by co-owners Lawrence R. Luhring and Roland J. Augustine. Check out the imposing back office where the big deals are made. The gallery's critical monographic exhibitions of Marcel Duchamp (1987), Gerhard Richter (1995) and Donald Judd (1999) put it firmly on the map. And it continues to show German painters like Gunther Forg and Sigmar Polke as well as international photographers and conceptual artists – Sophie Calle, Robert Gober and Rachel Whiteread among them. The Americans are Larry Clark, Paul McCarthy, Christopher Wool and Janine Antoni.

UPTOWN BARGAINS
9 Barney's Co-op
162

WHOLESALE FINE FOOD
10 Chelsea Market
75 Ninth Avenue

Originally the Nabisco factory and the birthplace of America's best-loved cookie, the Oreo, this building is today a buzzing market complex. Its street-block-sized interior houses a variety of specialty food shops that double as wholesale and retail outlets, while the upper floors contain old and new media firms. Architect Jeff Vandeberg and developer Irwin Cohen have created a playful atmosphere using features from the original factory, such as gears, pipes and machines as sculptural details along the central concourse.

11 Bottino
246 Tenth Avenue

After an evening of hopping from gallery-opening to gallery-opening, curators, artists and dealers flock to the Chelsea art scene's favorite feeding ground. The delicious Tuscan food satisfies the body, leaving the mind to ponder such critical issues as the future of landscape painting in contemporary art practice. Fifteen wines are offered by the glass to accompany dishes such as bocconcini of fresh mozzarella, tuna carpaccio and bresaola with arugula. At lunchtime ask for a table on the patio seating area, one of the finest outdoor oases in town.

12 Printed Matter
535 West 22nd Street

Printed Matter Inc. is the world's largest non-profit institution dedicated to the promotion of publications made by artists in a book-like format. After many years of operation in SoHo, Printed Matter moved its stock – limited-edition artworks, books, magazines and objects that blur both the definitions of and the boundaries between books and art – to new larger premises in the heart of the Chelsea art district. While the store still maintains its roots in traditional artist's books by the likes of Sol LeWitt, Lawrence Weiner and Ed Ruscha, it has recently begun to explore more contemporary interpretations of the genre including video tapes, CD-ROMS, multiples, as well as exhibition catalogs and monographs.

In addition to casting a net beyond the conventional boundary of art practice, Protetch specializes in drawings by architects. Since 1978, when he moved his gallery from Washington to New York, he has shown the work of Robert Venturi, Michael Graves, Zaha Hadid, Frank Gehry and Tadao Ando. Protetch also represents the estates of Frank Lloyd Wright and Buckminster Fuller. The gallery also has on its books such artists as Oliver Herring, David Reed, Thomas Nozkowski, Byron Kim, Iñigo Manglano-Ovalle and João Penalva. A recent show by Manglano filled the gallery with a fiberglass-and-titanium-alloy-foil scale model of a 20-mile-long (30-kilometer) cumulonimbus cloud entitled *Cloud Prototype No. 1, 2003.*

Take the elevator to the roof of this Gluckman Mayner-renovated building and start your visit with a bitter espresso in the small café you'll find there. Enter the Dan Graham "Rooftop Urban Park Project" glass sculpture and rotate 360 degrees, taking in the view of boats coming down the Hudson River, the immediate skyline of water towers and local gallerists' rooftop terraces. Then descend the staircase lined with Dan Flavin's fluorescent light pieces, floor by floor, viewing the large, long-running exhibitions by the likes of Lawrence Weiner, Ann Hamilton and Fred Sandback. Leave some time for browsing the playful ground-level bookstore with its tiled floor in boiled-sweet hues designed by Cuban artist Jorge Pardo.

15 Comme des Garçons

520 West 22nd Street

With an entrance like this – it looks like the gangplank to an alien spacecraft – it's hard to resist the lure of this veritable gallery of a shop, an appropriate environment for the structural architectonics of Rei Kawakubo's cult line of clothing. Future Systems, the experimental British firm that designed the space in 1998, kept the building's 19th-century façade intact and focused instead on creating the asymmetric tubular entrance made from aluminum.

A WORLD OF TEA

16 Wild Lily Tearoom

511A West 22nd Street

Take a break from art viewing and soothe your over-stimulated synapses with a nice cup of tea. Choose from a menu of more than 40 connoisseur-grade teas – from China, India, Taiwan and Japan – at this peaceful sanctuary designed by David Hu. You can sip your Tong Tin Oolong and nibble delicate Japanese sandwiches beside a small pond containing lily pads and four large goldfish.

DIGITAL-ARTS CENTER

17 Eyebeam Atelier

540 West 21st Street

Eyebeam was founded in 1996 by John S. Johnson to expose broad and diverse audiences to art and technology. The new media-art institution is currently in an interim exhibition and education space that in 2007 will open as a large Kubrickesque museum of art and technology designed by the digital-media-savvy architecture firm Diller + Scofidio. The new building will house a museum of art and technology, artist-in-residence ateliers, an education center, multimedia classrooms, a state-of-the-art theater and a digital archive. The facility will provide unprecedented production and exhibition opportunities for artists exploring new media in video, film and moving image art, DVD production, installation, 2D-3D digital imaging, net art and sound, and performance art forms.

ECCENTRIC TAPAS

18 El Quijote

226 West 23rd Street

This 60-year-old Spanish restaurant is the cafeteria – albeit one serving lobster and paella – for eccentric guests of the Chelsea hotel. The reason to stay, though, is the bar, which provides old-fashioned drinks, a comprehensive catalog of Quijote figurines and a vantage point over the dining room with its red banquettes filled with fascinating parties. Spend at least part of an evening propped at this bar savoring the musty aura of an old New York where waiters wear uniforms and bow ties and the fur- and fedora-wearing clientele still Brylcreem their hair and smoke cigarettes from silver cases.

PARKING-LOT-SIZE BAR

19 Lot 61

550 West 21st Street

This enormous loft bar and restaurant, designed by architect Rafael Viñoly, was one of the first to install site-specific art works. With a nod to the gallery district that it feeds and waters, Lot 61 spotted its interior with Damien Hirst, bedecked its ceilings with Jorge Pardo's hanging cylindrical lamps and announced its restrooms with Jim Hodge's fluorescent "Hello" light.

"I REMEMBER YOU WELL"

20 Hotel Chelsea

126

ART OF DISCO

21 Passerby

154

VANGUARD GALLERY

22 Gavin Brown's Enterprise

436 West 15th Street

This truly cutting-edge gallery is run by the British transplant Gavin Brown. A solid roster of young British and American artists includes Chris Ofili, Elizabeth Peyton and Rob Pruitt, Peter Doig and Udomsak Krisanamis, among others.

SWISS IMPORTS

23 Vitra Showroom

29 Ninth Avenue

These new offices and showroom for the furniture company Vitra were designed by architect of the moment Lindy Roy. Her conversion of a turn-of-the-century storage space is a study of sensual modernism. Three stories are connected by two slots that incorporate staircases, and large rubber-wrapped display surfaces that extend the floor area of the showroom on the second floor down into the first-floor retail space and the gallery below.

NEW ENGLAND ATMOSPHERE

25 The Red Cat

227 Tenth Avenue

The Red Cat's menu reflects the warmth and comfort of the restaurant's ambience with unpretentious, well-executed American bistro dishes. If you do not feel like making the commitment to a shell steak with yukon golds, fennel and aïoli with Cabernet sauce, then order some sides – definitely the parmesan French fries and red-hot rapini – to eat with a glass of excellent wine at the bar. The red-and-white barnwood interior has a New England feel but the addition of huge hanging candle lanterns from Morocco saves it from cute pastiche.

HEARTY FRENCH FARE

26 La Lunchonette

130 Tenth Avenue

La Lunchonette's friendly, slightly dishevelled interior is an inviting oasis and a welcome contrast to the desolate street it has inhabited since 1988. Jean-François Fraysse, the chef, and his wife, Melva Max, jointly own the place and serve up delicious French dishes such as lamb sausage with sautéed apples and pan-fried whole trout with wild mushrooms. On Sundays they feature live jazz.

LATE-NIGHT LOUNGE

27 APT

419 West 13th Street

Even though the secrecy surrounding this lounge bar styled as an apartment has dissipated somewhat, three years later, APT still does not exactly announce itself to West 13th Street. To enter you must first locate the metal warehouse outer door and then an inner one. And while the buzz may have moved on, the line-up of DJs such as Matthew Herbert and DJ Vadim and the iPod mixing sessions, where punters get a 3,000-song playlist and seven minutes on the decks, makes this India Mahdavi–designed space still fresh.

Even though you know this is a pitch-perfect simulation, a Disneyfication of a Parisian bistro, there are moments, on a weekday morning, for example, when – with an espresso, a newspaper plucked from the rack just inside the door and a sunlit breakfast spread on your window-side table – it feels great. Restaurateur Keith McNally, whose other restaurants include Lucky Strike, Pravda and Balthazar (p. 22), has surpassed himself with attention to detail in his conversion of a wholesale flower market into Pastis. Chefs Riad Nasr and Lee Hanson serve dishes inspired by hearty Provençal cuisine. Avoid the late-night invasion of up- and out-of-towners "slumming it" in the Meatpacking District and limit yourself to daytime and early evening visits.

Feng-shui master Tin Sun acted as consultant on design, construction and placement of elements in this transformation of a meat freezer into a meat market for the chic and sleek. The communal handbasin in the bathroom is a 140-pound (64-kg), 1-inch-thick (4-cm) slab of amber onyx mounted on a steel frame with stainless-steel taps affixed to a mirrored wall. Back in the restaurant a central inclining catwalk of coconut wood divides the large space into two different dining levels, each filled with polished rattan chairs and cream-colored, ostrich-leather banquettes.

31 Florent
69 Gansevoort Street

Florent, a diner that has been serving 24 hours of attitude a day since 1985, was given its graphic and visual form by the late Tibor Kalman of New York's famously irreverent design company M&Co. You come to this fluorescent-lit diner to talk politics, bounce wisecracks back and forth with the transsexual waitresses and, if you are a local, to open your mail with a mug of coffee at the Formica counter. Florent's forcefully liberal views on the changes in the neighborhood and the world are expressed with witty succinctness in white letters on a menu board. The food is inexpensive French bistro fare, like French onion soup, boudin noir and goat-cheese salad.

32 Jeffrey
449 West 14th Street

When Jeffrey first opened on the far west reaches of 14th Street in 1999 there were precious few other shops in the Meatpacking District. Taxicabs would emit fur-clad and Manolo-shod ladies who had to heel their way past skinned meat carcasses swinging from the doorways of meat lockers to get to the mini-department store's front door. Today the contrasts are less stark and the gasps are reserved solely for the dazzling footwear displays – Jeffrey Kalinsky, the store's owner, is a former shoe buyer at Barneys.

33 Magnolia Bakery

401 Bleecker Street

The cupcakes under 1950s bell jars in the window of this chaotic, old-fashioned bakeshop are what people travel from all over town for. Pink, yellow and brown butter icing is slapped inches-thick on to the palm-sized sponge cakes and then topped with lurid sprinkles. You can take them away in boxes for parties but most people choose to linger with their prize in the sugary steam of the café or on a small bench outside.

"WE LOVE MARC JACOBS"

34 Marc Jacobs

172

DRESSING UP

35 Diane von Furstenberg

385 West 12th Street

For classically sexy silk jersey wrap dresses, in her signature prints and solid colors, head to Diane von Furstenberg's shimmering store in the far reaches of the West Village. The wraps, along with ruched tops, slim-fitting, ultra-suede pants and coordinating accessories, are presented in a store designed by BE Partners and Bill Katz. The wall and ceiling treatment consists of plaster spotted with flush, 4-inch (10-cm) mirror disks and halogen lamps. The dressing rooms, in the center of the store, are enclosed in a circle of ceiling-to-floor white silk draperies and the Furstenberg dotted logo is deployed on sandblasted-glass pivot doors that separate the retail and event spaces.

TRAVEL KIT

36 Flight 001

96 Greenwich Avenue

Brad John and John Sencion have cornered the *Wallpaper**-toting, wanderlust market with their mod West Village travel boutique. For real adventurers there are travel guides, leather passport holders, backpacks, wash bags and Braun travel clocks. For armchair ones there are globes, retro watches and coffee-table books. Dario C. Antonio's 1999 design for the store includes rubber flooring, a glowing back wall and universal travel symbols in powder blue for decorative detail.

BEER AND BURGERS

37 Corner Bistro

140

ESSENCE OF JAZZ

38 Smalls

183 West 10th Street

Smalls is a Greenwich Village basement jazz den famed for its riotous early morning jam sessions (it's open until 8 am). Juices and teas are served at the bar, and although there is no liquor license, you can bring your own libations. Mitch Borden is the hands-on owner of the place: His special offer is $10 for 10 hours of jazz. Don't expect to leave before dawn.

OLD-FASHIONED DELIGHTS

39 Li-Lac Chocolates

120 Christopher Street

With 5,000 moulds in all shapes and sizes, the chocolatiers at this tiny, ribbon-tied box of a shop are ready to make your chocolate fantasies come true. Established by a French family in the 1920s, Li-Lac Chocolates has been in the same 1883 building ever since. It's a favorite destination for the Villagers, despite long lines during holidays.

GAS-LIT PHARMACY

40 C.O. Bigelow Apothecaries

414 Sixth Avenue

This 162-year-old apothecary is still outfitted with its original 1838 wood shelving, tiles, ceiling mouldings and gas chandeliers. Old Delftware drug jars and historic prescriptions are interspersed with Bigelow's merchandise, which encompasses an in-house line of perfumed oils, its Alchemy line of make-up and old American standards, such as Calgon and Ivory. Illustrious former customers include Samuel L. Clemens, better known as Mark Twain, who, for a while, lived around the corner at 21 Fifth Avenue.

HIDDEN EATERY

41 Grange Hall

30 Commerce Street

From an organic brunch to a late-night drink at the bar, this cosy West Village restaurant is a delight. Partly because of the secluded charm of the street, a rarely used dogleg that connects Hudson Street and Seventh Avenue, and partly thanks to the charming bar staff, it's often hard to tear yourself away. If you do, note the nearby early-19th-century buildings, including the Cherry Lane Theater next door. It was founded by Edna St Vincent Millay in 1924 and was housed in an 1836 brewery to stage surreal works, such as *Waiting for Godot*, which was premiered here.

Gramercy Park
East Village
Lower East Side
Lower Manhattan

This exploration of the eastern flank of Manhattan begins at the island's well-fed right thigh and ends at its en pointe toe. In historical terms the journey runs counter to the city's evolution. Beginning with the once-far-uptown settlement of Gramercy Square, where the wealthiest knickerbockers congregated, it continues through the slums of the immigrant staging posts of the Lower East Side and finally arrives in the oldest part of New York, which was, from 1626 until it overcrowded in the mid-19th century, New York's chaotic center.

Gramercy Park is the centerpiece of a historic district of tree-shaded streets lined with a variety of 19th-century residences, from 1840s row houses and brownstones to Victorian-era Queen Annes and neo-Gothics, which lend the area a particular gentility.

The East Village's history starts circa 1960 when it branched off from the Lower East Side as an area self-defined by its countercultural activity centered on a few coffee houses and clubs around St. Mark's Place. The area was plagued with drug-related crime throughout the 1970s and 1980s and provided the gritty backdrop for an exciting art and punk-rock scene. The Giuliani-administered clean-up of Tompkins Square Park in 1992 brought a trail of French bistros and media types in its wake, pushing its original residents and those who arrived too late to the southeast. These pioneers found themselves in a Lower East Side both stained and bespangled by its longstanding role as the immigrant gateway for the rest of New York. The first wave of arrivals took place throughout the 19th century, when political events in Europe and anti-Chinese sentiment on the West Coast fanned the sails of boatloads of settlers towards New York. A century later, in the 1960s, following a relaxation of immigration laws, streams of new colors, languages, religions and cultures formed vibrant and sometimes violent eddies in the area. The most recent flood of new blood is largely Puerto Rican, Dominican and young white musicians and artists. Ludlow and Orchard were the scenes of a severe attack of hipification in the 1990s, and Clinton and Rivington are the ongoing sites of more recent and, thankfully, more considered creative intrusion.

Continuing south and further back in time you arrive at the narrow, tangled streets laid out by 17th-century Dutch settlers, when the city was still known as New Amsterdam. Among the closely packed top-heavy financial and Old World corporate centers and smoky, back-alley taverns down the crooked lanes that resisted the imposition of the 19th-century grid, it's easy to lose your sense of time and space — that is, until you emerge into the southernmost territory of the island, where a boat ride or walk across the Brooklyn Bridge provides an exhilarating view of the city.

CLASSIC SANCTUARY

1 Gramercy Park Hotel

GOTHIC ARCHITECTURE, MEMBERS ONLY

2 National Arts Club

15 Gramercy Park South

Built in 1845, this building has housed the National Arts Club and its members – the first of whom included Theodore Roosevelt and Woodrow Wilson – since 1906. Its original flat-front, iron-grilled appearance matched the style of the houses still maintained on the west side of Gramercy Park. But in the 1880s, the mansion's owner, Samuel Tilden, hired Calvert Vaux – one of the designers of Central Park – to bring the façade up to tempo with the current trend for High Victorian Gothic style. Vaux added bay windows, polychromatic brickwork and Gothic ornamentation. During exhibitions and events, when the public is admitted, you can see the stained-glass ceilings that John LaFarge created for the inside of the mansion and the Italian carved fireplaces. You may even see Martin Scorsese, Ethan Hawke, Dennis Hopper and Uma Thurman, who are among the club's current members.

GREENMARKET SALADS AND DOUBLE-CHOCOLATE COOKIES

3 City Bakery

3 West 18th Street

Visit City Bakery for a sublime chocolate experience that might include a "shot" of viscous dark chocolate scooped from a constantly churning vat or a huge double-chocolate cookie freshly baked by pastry chef and owner, Maury Rubin. For lunch, this airy café, frequented by designers and photographers from the surrounding Flatiron district, has the best seasonal salad counter in town, assembled by chef Ilene Rosen. The Bakery holds bizarre food festivals throughout the year, such as the "City Bakery State Fair" in July when the otherwise urbane space undergoes a country makeover with a carpet of hay, a picket fence and gingham-clad girls serving corn dogs and farmer's lemonade.

ALE AND WINGS SINCE 1864

4 Pete's Tavern

129 East 18th Street

The living heart of Irving Place is an Irish saloon that has been continuously serving "grocery and grog" since 1864. It even stayed open during Prohibition, disguised as a flower shop. It is said that one of the regulars, O. Henry, wrote *Gift of the Magi* at the first booth by the door during 1902. Today the bar has an Italian-American menu, three TV screens and a loyal crowd of after-work drinkers. Pete's own 1864 Original Ale is still drawn from old porcelain taps set in the 30-foot-long (9-meter) rosewood bar.

NEW AMERICAN DIY

5 Craft

A GOURMET AMERICAN COUNTRY REFUGE

6 Gramercy Tavern

42 East 20th Street

For some New American gastronomic indulgence, consider Tom Colicchio's market menu at the well-established and -loved Gramercy Tavern. It involves a taste of almost everything on the exceptional menu and reaches a crescendo with three of Claudia Fleming's exceptional desserts that might include a mascarpone cream Napoleon with rhubarb compote and strawberries. For a less expensive alternative there is the handsome bar in the festive Tavern Room at the front of the rustic-themed restaurant. With more than 85 selections, the cheese course ranks as one of the city's finest. Order a selection of three, six or ten as a dessert, or sample with wine at the bar. The service throughout is impeccable; service staff tell you how dishes taste, not just what's in them.

WHARTONESQUE RETREAT

7 The Inn at Irving Place

INDIAN-INFUSED CUISINE

8 Tabla

11 Madison Avenue

Young Bombay-born chef Floyd Cardoz fuses American and Indian cuisines at this flamboyantly designed restaurant in the Art Déco Metropolitan Life Tower. Dishes such as tandoori quail with black-pepper glaze, taro-dusted halibut with white beans, and scallops in mustard-oil-red-pepper coulis have earned Cardoz the adoring attention of New York food critics. The richly colored curvy space features a suspended second floor around a "viewing well." Here you can snack on grape-pine-nut and tomato-kalonji chutneys or guacamole with toasted cumin on a variety of breads. The restaurant's owner is Danny Meyer, whose other smash successes are Union Square Café, Gramercy Tavern and Eleven Madison Park. For a taste of his style to go, try a gourmet-prepared hot dog from his stand positioned outside Eleven Madison Park.

EARLY STEEL-FRAME SKYSCRAPER
9 Flatiron Building
175 Fifth Avenue

Daniel H. Burnham's iconic building was, in 1902 – when it was built to fill a triangular-shaped site where Broadway crosses Fifth Avenue – one of New York's first skyscrapers. Today the steel-framed structure, clad in panels of terracotta and limestone, gives its nickname to a district colonized by photography shops, design organizations – AIGA and the Art Directors' Club both have public exhibition galleries within a few picas of the building's base – production houses and design studios. You will find many photographers – perhaps inspired by the legendary shots of Edward Steichen and Alfred Stieglitz – setting up their tripods in the traffic island to the north of the Flatiron.

NO-FRILLS BEAUTY PRODUCTS
10 Kiehl's
169

INDIAN-SPICED FABRICS
11 Alpana Bawa
41 Grand Street, 70 East 1st Street

Punjab-born Alpana Bawa threads her Indian heritage into the fabric of her vividly colored and immaculately tailored clothing line. Her original construction methods and use of color have earned her "darling" status among fashion critics. Pink and lilac tanks embroidered with leaves and vines and beaded evening gowns are among the favorites of her female fans. Men, too, can flaunt in architecturally inspired colored or patterned shirts.

JAPANESE NETHERWORLD
12 Decibel
240 East 9th Street

From the moment you descend the steps and ring the buzzer for this basement bar you're submerged in a Japanese netherworld. Low lighting, an idiosyncratic soundtrack and kooky Japanese bar staff combine to create an atmosphere that can vary from subdued to wild in the space of one evening. The wooden bar in the front room conceals a den in the back for some seated sake and appetizer consumption. The okonomiyaki (Japanese pancake) is a house favorite.

CLANDESTINE COCKTAILS
13 Angel's Share
156

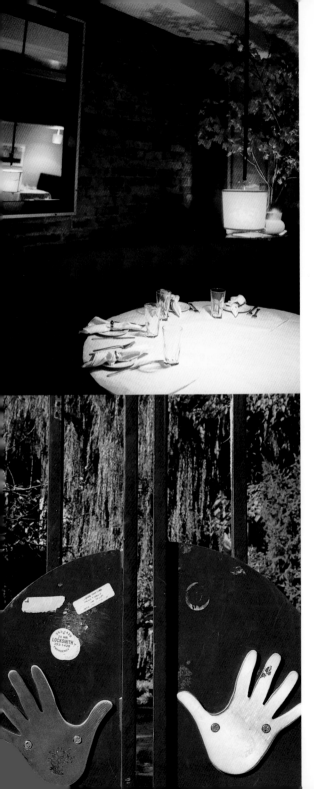

BEER, SPIT AND SAWDUST

14 McSorley's Old Ale House

151

AFTER-HOURS SALON

15 First

87 First Avenue

Chef and owner Sam DeMarco's late-night salon provides a creative contemporary American menu as you put the world to rights at 2:00 a.m. Over 30 varieties of vodkatinis are served in three sizes of carafe submerged in a bowl of ice with a chilled glass and can be accompanied by lollipop buffalo wings.

QUIRKY CHARM

16 Prune

143

URBAN PASTORAL

17 Community Garden

East 6th Street and Avenue B

Where once a garbage- and weed-filled lot stood at the corner of East 6th Street and Avenue B, there now thrives a lush and magical community garden, replete with wisteria-creeping arbors. A 37-foot (11-meter) tower built by a lifelong neighborhood resident from material discarded by local people is the centerpiece of the garden's cultivated plots and shady paths. The garden, both the quirkiest and prettiest of the many fenced-in patches of land planted with trees, bushes and flower beds in the Lower East Side, is open to the public on Saturday and Sunday afternoons and for its numerous evening events.

BOXY BAR WITH GOOD BEATS

18 Standard

158 First Avenue

Bring your own crowd to the Standard Bar and Listening Room and, since the pocket-sized space feels full with a dozen people in it, you'll have your own party. Nightly, different DJs preside over the turntables in the corner. On "Urban Foldz Mondays," for example, DJ Jedi delivers "deep beats, nu-skool breaks, electro, minimal tech, trip hop and all-around underground goodness." The bar's design is minimal. Its few features include storefront windows that are partially frosted, a square epoxy-resin bar, rubber and steel stools and gently glowing backlit panels on the north wall.

MOBY'S TEASHOP
19 Teany

CAVIAR AND PICKLES
20 Russ & Daughters
179 East Houston Street

Joel Russ began serving schmaltz herring in a barrel and salt-cured lox at this location in the 1920s. His daughters – Hattie, Ida and Anne – joined him at the spotless white-tile counter in the 1940s. Now in its fourth generation of ownership, the delicatessen, which the Smithsonian Institution deems to be "part of New York's cultural heritage," is still going strong. People come from all over the city for gleaming beluga, osetra and sevruga caviar, smoked sturgeon, herring and salmon, as well as candied fruits and nuts. Just outside the door, you can check the time by the scrambled numbers on the clock on top of the Red Square apartment building, designed by Tibor Kalman.

"I'LL HAVE WHAT SHE'S HAVING"
21 Katz's Deli

FRESH KICKS
22 Alife Rivington Club and Alife
- Alife Rivington Club, 158 Rivington Street
- Alife, 178 Orchard Street

You have to buzz at an unmarked door to be admitted to the wood-paneled and red-carpeted members' club for sworn-in sneaker heads. Top-lit vitrines display vintage Dunks, Jordans and Air Force-1s as well as Adidas originals. A sloping shelf exhibits the store's own line, Ritefoot, as well as a select line-up of contemporary sought-afters. Around the corner you'll find Alife, a storefront that poses variously as a gallery – featuring work that teeters enjoyably between the genres of graffiti, graphic design and art – and a store – for all your streetwear and accessory needs, such as rare Japanese action figures and limited-edition Nixon watches.

CANDIES GALORE
23 Economy Candy
108 Rivington Street

This cluttered candy warehouse has been selling jawbreakers, strawberry shoelaces and Atomic Fireballs a penny a piece since 1937. The store's owner, Jerry Cohen, will climb a ladder to reach your favorite jar from the floor-to-ceiling shelves.

24 TG170

170 Ludlow Street

Terry Gillis has launched many a fashion career from her pioneering store at 170 Ludlow. Her labels of choice include Pixie Yates, Living Doll, United Bamboo, Ulla Johnson and Liz Collins. Accessories include bags that range from the beat-up messenger functionality of Freitag to the delicate whimsy of purses made from vintage kimono fabrics. In the T-shirt department is Supersonic's hot-dog-print muscle-tee, in addition to perennial favorites from Petite Bateau.

IMMIGRANT LIFE

25 Lower East Side Tenement Museum

90 Orchard Street

This fascinating museum is made up of a series of tenement buildings, accessible by guided tour only, that give you an often-eerie insight into aspects of immigrant life in the late 19th century. The Lower East Side is referred to as the "gateway to America," for the vast number of immigrants it has housed (often in appalling conditions) over the years. The tenement at 90 Orchard, for example, was home to an estimated 7,000 people from more than 20 nations between 1863 and 1935. Its apartments are carefully restored to allow interpretation of the lives of the actual residents from different historical periods who lived here.

AVANT-GARDE FASHION

26 Seven

180 Orchard Street

Joseph Quartana and John Demas preside over this incubator of homegrown progressive design talent. Young independent New York fashion designers, such as As Four and Tess Giberson, are represented in this concrete-floored, clean white space (designed by Demas), along with the new constructions and deconstructions of Sophia Kokosalaki, Martin Margiela and Tim Van Steenbergen.

ROMANTIC GERMAN SYNAGOGUE

27 Angel Orensanz Foundation

172 Norfolk Street

This synagogue was commissioned from Berlin architect Alexander Seltzer in 1849 by members of the German Jewish community, who arrived in Manhattan in the 1840s. In 1986 the sculptor Angel Orensanz bought the decaying structure and saved it from demolition. Now the neo-Gothic central space, with 50-foot-high (15-meter) ceilings and ringed by ornate balconies, is rented out for spectacular candle-lit parties and cultural events such as Alexander McQueen's first American fashion show and Rainer Werner Fassbinder's *City, Garbage and Death*.

LAIDBACK MOROCCAN LOUNGE

28 Kush

183 Orchard Street

The Moroccan-owned and -themed Kush is a languorous nightlife spot amid a frenzy of nocturnal activity up and down Orchard and Ludlow Streets. Once your eyes have adjusted to the colored candlelight emitted through ornate tin chandeliers and wall sconces, you'll spot your own cushioned dark corner. Lean back and puff on a hookah while belly dancers (on Tuesday nights) undulate to the rhythms of Souren Baronian's Middle Eastern trio.

GOURMAND'S STRIP

29 Clinton Street

- 71 Clinton Fresh Food, no. 71
- aka Café, no. 49
- WD–50, no. 50

When they set up their restaurant on a deserted stretch of Clinton Street in 1999, owners Dewey Dufresne and Janet Nelson thought they would be "opening a restaurant that would be moderately priced and have a nice local atmosphere." Instead, thanks to a combination of the restaurant's contemporary design – exposed brick, vinyl banquettes and orange and green walls on the inside and an aluminum and glass frontage – the recent "hipification" of Clinton Street and the stunning creations of rising star chef Willie Dufresne shot right out of the "neighborhood" category into the stratosphere. Today, although Willie Dufresne cooks at his own restaurant, WD-50, which is across the road in a converted bodega, and has left No. 71 in the hands of his former sous-chef, Matthew Reguin, many of his original creations are still on the menu. The goat-cheese tart topped with sliced potatoes and dotted with rich applewood-smoked bacon, still stuns the critics. Soups, sandwiches, and empanadas are the staples of AKA café, No.71's smaller, more casual offshoot, just a couple of doors up the street.

GOOD LIBATIONS

30 Good World Barber Shop

150

31 New York Stock Exchange
8 Broad Street

This marble temple encases one of the most important nerve centers of the global economy. Built in 1903 by George B. Post, the edifice's two-story base and powerful Corinthian columns signify permanence and power. Although visitors are currently not able to view the frenetic trading floor, the Exchange is an appropriate starting point for a short exploration into the district's fusion of finance and power-architecture. The Museum of American Financial History (24 Broadway) tells a history of Wall Street through its displays of ancient ticker-tape machines, telegraphs and trading tables. If you book well ahead, you can also tour the Federal Reserve Bank of New York (33 Liberty Street), which holds the nation's largest store of gold. The limestone-clad skyscraper of Bank of New York (1 Wall Street and Broadway) was built in 1932 and its banking hall is an Art Déco feast of gold, orange and red mosaic tiles.

32 Skyscraper Museum
39 Battery Place

At the base of the Ritz Carlton Hotel in Battery Park, the long-migratory Skyscraper Museum has found a permanent home, due to open in late 2003. Skyscraper titans Skidmore, Owings & Merrill have designed the brand-new facility, which will contain one gallery devoted to the evolution of New York's commercial skyline and another for changing shows that explore aspects of high-rise building. An after-museum cocktail in the hotel's 14th-floor Rise bar affords clear views across the harbor to the Statue of Liberty. Alternatively, a sea-breezy walk across Battery Park takes you to the Staten Island Ferry terminal, from where you can ride to and from Staten Island (about 30 minutes each way) taking in close-up views of the Statue of Liberty, engineered by Alexandre Gustave Eiffel, on the way out and a southerly perspective of the high rises of Lower Manhattan, on the return, all for no charge.

ROMANCING THE BRIDGE
33 Brooklyn Bridge and Bridge Café
279 Water Street

A decorative pressed-tin ceiling, ample windows displaying the Manhattan-bound arches of the Brooklyn Bridge, and a setting in one of the city's oldest food-serving buildings are just a few features that make the delightfully snug and, in the evening, positively romantic Bridge Café worth a visit. Once sated, walk the wooden platform that traverses the outer edge of Brooklyn Bridge, that lyrical 1883 construction of soaring steel-wire cables and neo-Gothic towers that was the largest suspension bridge in the world and the first to be constructed in steel. Beneath the supporting pier on the Brooklyn side of the East River, in a high barrel-vaulted space, is the Brooklyn Bridge Anchorage, one of the city's most exciting experimental music and art venues. Before returning, walk among the early- and mid-19th-century brownstones and brick houses, once the homes of prosperous ship captains and now

populated by wealthy filmmakers and writers. Stroll the Brooklyn Heights Promenade between Cranberry and Remsen Streets for a view of Lower Manhattan's skyline, especially magical at sunset.

A COLONIAL INN
34 Fraunces Tavern
54 Pearl Street

In the final days of the Revolutionary War, the tavern served as George Washington's residence, and it was in the Long Room that he delivered his farewell to the officers of the Continental army on 4 December 1783 before returning to his residence at Mount Vernon. In 1904 the historic significance of the then-decaying building was realized, and it was reconstructed to look like a late-18th-century inn. Today Wall Street traders frequent the colonial-style street-level dining room, and there is a museum on the upper floors, if a little dusty, that has a certain charm.

Midtown

Midtown is New York at its most vertiginous and luminous. On street level, the traffic lights turn and the crowds cross the grids like clockwork. Overhead, the lofty ambitions of mid-century Modernist architecture reach towards infinity. From broad-shouldered corporate headquarters along the "Park Avenue Corridor" to the designer flagships of Fifth Avenue, and from the fiber-optic stars that twinkle on the ceiling of Grand Central Station to the diode-cacophony of Times Square, Midtown condenses and amplifies the energy of the city in ways that are both exhausting and exhilarating.

Among the pillars of commerce are some pioneers of 1950s "glass box" architecture, including the Seagram Building by Mies van der Rohe and Philip Johnson, and the newly restored Lever House by Skidmore, Owings & Merrill (SOM), which was the city's first building to be constructed entirely from steel and glass. The postmodern response came in the improbable forms of Philip Johnson's "Lipstick Building," Edward Barnes's black granite prism for IBM and Johnson's Chippendale breakfront top for AT&T (now owned by Sony).

Grand Central Station, designed in 1913 and newly emerged from a decade-long renovation program, combines an extraordinary feat of urban planning — multilevel circulation for cars, trains, subways and pedestrians — and magnificent Beaux Arts architecture. The terminal was preserved after many years of decline, thanks to a campaign spearheaded by Jacqueline Onassis. The romantic revival Pennsylvania Station further southwest of Grand Central was not so lucky. The 1910 building, a noble gateway to the city, designed by McKim, Mead & White, was unceremoniously torn down in the 1960s and replaced by a nondescript cat-flap of an entryway. Now, the General Post Office across the street is being transformed by SOM into a new Penn Station with a soaring arch of steel and glass.

In the mid- to late-19th century, Midtown was the most fashionable residential neighborhood in New York. The Vanderbilts alone had four mansions between 34th and 59th Streets. Today, little remains of this genteel past except for the two exquisite buildings that now house Cartier and Versace. The new occupants of Fifth Avenue are flagship shops — Tiffany, Calvin Klein, Gucci — and upmarket department stores — Henri Bendel, Bergdorf Goodman, Barneys — emitting their distilled essences via the streams of branded shopping bags that flow up and down the thoroughfare. Midtown is also the center of the city's media and publishing industries. At the power-lunch hour, when television, magazine and web executives sally out to Michael's or The Four Seasons, the river of shopping totes absorbs tributaries of briefcases and laptop cases from which protrude furled copies of *The New York Times*, *The New Yorker* or *Harper's*.

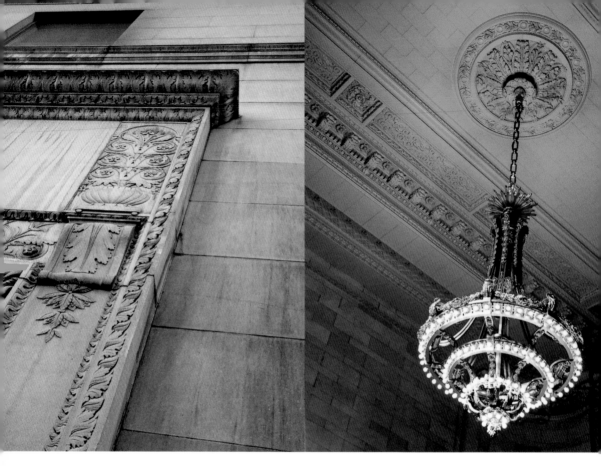

THE GILDED AGE

1 The Morgan Library

29 East 36th Street

By 1906, J. Pierpont Morgan, banker, philanthropist and collector, needed a building to house his amazing collection of rare books, Old Master drawings and autographed manuscripts. Charles McKim gave him an Italian Renaissance-style palazzo with three magnificent rooms epitomizing America's Age of Elegance. Among the highlights of the library, located in Murray Hill, you can find three copies of the Gutenberg Bible, Charles Dickens's manuscript of *A Christmas Carol*, Henry David Thoreau's journals and Thomas Jefferson's letters to his daughter Martha. There is a pleasant courtyard café, but if you're in the mood for something stronger, duck down into the dark hideaway of the Andrée Putman–designed Morgans Bar, beneath Morgans Hotel at 237 Madison Ave and 37th Street.

MONUMENT TO MOVEMENT

2 Grand Central Terminal

42nd Street

While this 1913 Beaux Arts terminal is a thrilling point of departure for a train journey, there's plenty to do here without buying a ticket. Spend a while watching the 300,000 commuters bend deftly around obstacles en masse like schools of fish that never collide. Watch as the light floods through the magnificent clerestory windows – not always as dramatic as the moment in 1934 when Hal Morey took his famous photo of it. Look at the restored celestial-blue ceiling as it winks with its fibre-optic and gold-leaf constellations. Finally, visit the Campbell Apartment, a truly bizarre cocktail lounge, which from 1923 to 1941 was the private office and salon of New York Central Railroad trustee, John Campbell. He had the room designed to resemble a 13th-century Florentine palazzo with stained-glass windows and an intricately carved, timbered ceiling.

OYSTER VAULT

3 **Oyster Bar at Grand Central Station**

URBAN GARDEN GEM

4 **Paley Park**

5 East 53rd Street

This delightful tiny vest-pocket park dating from 1967 uses the attributes of its intensely urban setting to its advantage, a genuine oasis in a concrete jungle. A massive waterfall obliterates the sound of the traffic, and the dappled shade of 17 honey-locust trees draws people in for a peaceful lunch. Designed by Zion and Breen Associates, the park was funded by William Paley, former chairman of CBS, who was involved in every aspect of the design, right down to the selection of the hot dog stand. Paley Park was a favorite spot of urban theorist William "Holly" Whyte, who, when the park first opened, used time-lapse photography to show how people used public urban spaces.

THE ART OF REFINEMENT

5 **Gucci**

685 Fifth Avenue

This flagship's interior created by SoHo Grand architect Bill Sofield is a suitably lean and glistening setting for Tom Ford's super-sexy designs for the Italian fashion house. Materials such as rosewood, Lucite, lacquer, travertine, glass, polished stainless steel and mohair are used to create contrasting textural effects throughout the store. The ground level, which is devoted to handbags, small leather goods, eyewear and jewelry, is dominated by a dramatic, double-height space offset by a proliferation of Neutra-inspired horizontal and cantilevered forms. Clothing hangs on an adjustable system suspended from the ceilings and is silhouetted against illuminated wall panels, which, according to the designer, "show the subtleties of fabric and detailing to great effect."

6 New York Public Library

Fifth Avenue and 42nd Street

Completed in 1911, Carrère and Hastings Library, designed to house the collection of bibliophile and real-estate millionaire John Astor, is a masterpiece of Beaux Arts design. If you take a tour, a docent will lead you around a dozen or so of the rooms, including one containing Charles Dickens's writing desk. Alternatively you can wander at your leisure through the rows of researchers in the finely restored Rose Main Reading Room or stand in the Astor Hall lobby, seemingly carved from one giant piece of marble, and contemplate the inherent contradictions of an institution built for public access yet financed by robber barons of the late 19th century. The library also puts on many excellent exhibitions, and lunch can be had within paces of its magnificent steps – the Bryant Park Grill is right behind the library in a park that shows outdoor movie classics in the summer, and Ilo is a gourmet restaurant in the Bryant Park Hotel on East 40th Street.

SUPERMODEL HANGOUT

7 Cellar Bar

156

ART DÉCO SKYSCRAPER

8 Chrysler Building

405 Lexington Avenue

New York's best-loved and most glorious skyscraper is an Art Déco classic. Even if you've seen it a thousand times before, there are moments when it can still take your breath away. When a glancing sunray lifts your gaze to its Nirosta stainless-steel crown – modeled after a Chrysler radiator grille – or at dusk, when its triangular-shaped windows set in layered scallops begin to emit their white light, Van Alen's optimistic vision of the future holds true. You see the 1930 building in your mind's eye, like all of New York, from afar. An up-close visit, however, with your head tilted back, rewards you with a different perspective. Automobile-themed, handcrafted ornaments such as brickwork cars are at the base of the tower and eagles in place of gargoyles lean out at the building's 61st floor. The lofty crown jewel of the building – the Cloud Room, a 1930s speak-easy with pink marble bathrooms and a gleaming bar of Bavarian wood – is out of bounds, unless you have the gall of tour operator Timothy "Speed" Levitch in the documentary *The Cruise*. Until it is restored you will have to content yourself with the lobby, lined with red African marble, the murals and the marquetry on the elevator doors.

INTERNATIONAL TERRITORY

9 United Nations Headquarters

First Avenue at 46th Street

In 1947 an international group of architects convened in New York under the supervision of Wallace K. Harrison. Their mission was to produce a home for the newly formed United Nations but, thanks to Le Corbusier's loudly voiced vision, the end result was much more than that. The United Nations complex is nothing short of an architectural icon signaling both modernity and world peace. The optimism of the project was reflected in Hitchcock's lens as he lingeringly drew down the green-tinted glass façade of the Secretariat Building in the opening scene of his 1959 movie *North by Northwest*. Today the interior has a faded quality captured most poignantly by Adam Bartos's photographs in the book *International Territory: The UN 1945–1995*. You can dine with diplomats in the Delegates Dining Room, the windows of which give capacious views across the East River. The term international cuisine is taken very literally at this lunch buffet and every month features a different country's national cuisine.

POWER-DRINKING

10 Four Seasons Bar

159

NEW STANDARDS

11 Brasserie

137

BESPOKE ARTS

12 Steven Salen Tailors

18 East 53rd Street

A suite of wood-paneled rooms is the genteel site for this old-fashioned, no-nonsense tailors' business. The establishment was once patronized by Ernest Hemingway, upon the recommendation of his friend Gerald Murphy – the dapper artist upon whom F. Scott Fitzgerald based the character Dick Driver in *Tender Is the Night*. Murphy advised that the tailors was a "Very good reliable old New York house, no chi-chi." Whether you want an entire wardrobe custom-made for summering on the Riviera or a minor alteration, you can trust a tailor that in 1933 placed an advertisement in *Fortune* magazine reading, "As formal clothes are conspicuous whatever the occasion, it is essential that such clothes be cut only by those who understand the basic laws of dress, otherwise the individual is in grave danger of paying a goodly sum for an entirely unsuitable outfit."

USEFUL AND FANCY ARTICLES

13 Tiffany & Co.

727 Fifth Avenue

You can't approach the door of Tiffany & Co. without picturing Holly Golightly in her Givenchy gown, dark glasses and pearls, sipping coffee and nibbling on a Danish, and gazing wistfully at the treasures displayed in the window. If, like Holly in *Breakfast at Tiffany's*, your "reds" can be soothed away by a small, pale-blue box, then head for this Fifth Avenue emporium of expensive jewels. Established in 1837, the store enjoyed its heyday at the turn of the 20th century, when Louis Comfort Tiffany, son of the store's founder, began designing his famous lamps and decadent Art Nouveau jewelry and enamels. Today the star designers are Elsa Peretti and Paloma Picasso.

MIDTOWN MERRIMENT

14 King Cole Bar and Lounge

155

ARCHITECTURE CENTER

15 Municipal Art Society and Urban Center Books

457 Madison Avenue

The northern wing of the 120-year-old landmark Villard House contains the ornate lobby and the Villard Bar and Lounge of the Palace Hotel, as well as a collection of architecturally focused organizations. The Municipal Art Society of New York champions excellence in urban design and planning and the preservation of the best of New York's past. Urban Center Books is a bookstore piled high, on the central table and the floor, with literature on urban affairs, architecture and the allied arts. It holds regular architecture-related talks, events and exhibits.

CLEAN LINES

16 Linda Dresner

484 Park Avenue

Since 1985 Linda Dresner has been exhibiting clean-lined haute couture in her Park Avenue boutique. She is credited with being the first to bring Jil Sander's minimal work to New York. Incidentally, the Hamburg-based designer finally has her own New York store at 11 East 57th Street. New York magazine described Michael Gabellini's pale, refined interior for Linda Dresner as an "iceberg space" when it first opened in an architectural climate more geared to the appreciation of the post-Modernism of Michael Graves, say, than the extreme minimalism that this store embodies. With light as an essential component of the architecture, Gabellini used expensive natural materials such as limestone, white marble, black granite, black macassar ebony and nickel silver to create an eminently luxurious environment for equally high-caliber garments.

THE SKYSCRAPER REVISITED

17 LVMH Tower
19–21 East 57th Street

You need to stand on the south side of 57th Street to be able to admire the Louis Vuitton–Moët Hennessy Tower as it twists and folds its way up 23 stories high. French architect Christian de Portzamparc's design proves that, contrary to popular belief, New York's stringent zoning laws do not inhibit experimentation. Making use of three types of glass – clear glass, green glass with ceramic frit, and a white, low-iron glass with a sandblasted geometric pattern – Portzamparc describes his tower, with its transparent faceted skin, as homage to the city of glass. A Christian Dior store takes up the building's first two levels, and elevators give access to the administrative offices of Louis Vuitton and its affiliates on floors 3 to 22. Topping the tower is a spectacular glass cube where a 30-foot-high (9-meter) penthouse is the scene of lavish fashion shows and parties.

TEMPLE OF COMMERCIAL COOL

18 Calvin Klein
654 Madison Avenue

The Calvin Klein flagship store is a vast minimalist temple. The store's architect, John Pawson, considered space as one of the most luxurious of the materials he had to play with and he used it liberally. "It's a modern idea of luxury, to give people space," he says. His other theme was white. Many shades of it are used throughout the interior, like the materialization of an Icelandic dictionary entry for "snow." The site was once a bank and Pawson retained the exterior Ionic pilasters and slid between them enormous vertical panes of glass framed with limestone.

ANTICIPATING THE GUGGENHEIM

19 Mercedes-Benz Showroom
430 Park Avenue

This tiny showroom designed by Frank Lloyd Wright in 1954 can hold only five cars. They are positioned around a circular, sloping ramp that was a small forerunner of the Guggenheim Museum's rotunda, some 30 blocks up the street. The geometry of the large circular mirror in the ceiling exploits the three-pointed star of Mercedes-Benz.

20 Algonquin Hotel

59 West 44th Street

The hotel lobby is the site of the historic Round Table at which, during the heady 1920s, Dorothy Parker pitted her acerbic wit against fellow literati. The Oak Room puts on cabaret acts every night except Monday. But it is the smaller round tables of the utterly unfashionable and slightly dusty Blue Bar that you should head for. Its walls are decorated with the artwork of long-time Algonquin regular Al Hirschfeld. Its uniformed waiters with their inscrutable demeanors serve pub fare and well-made Martinis. Just remember Parker's wisdom on that subject: "I like to have a Martini/Two at the very most/After three I'm under the table/After four I'm under the host."

21 Times Square

42nd Street and Broadway

New York's most famous square, in fact an elongated intersection where Broadway crosses Fifth Avenue, was named after *The New York Times* when it moved to the site in the early 1900s. The newspaper's building was the world's first to display a zipper sign on which the paper posted election returns in 1928. Ever since, the buildings around the square have been engaged in competition for ownership of bigger and brighter signs. Little Lulu and her Kleenex box, the puffing Camel smoker and the various neon displays that once wowed the passing public now seem like quaint exercises in restraint since the recent profusion of kinetic video monitors and jumbo digital displays that have enough candlepower to be visible at noon. Also of note in the Square is the US Armed Forces Recruiting Station designed by Architecture Research Office.

Join Russian intellectuals, writers, artists and sometimes Mikhail Baryshnikov (who is part-owner and frequent patron) at the long smoky bar for a warming shot of horseradish vodka. Rousing traditional Russian folk tunes that are often sung around the piano may persuade you to stay. Pick from a rainbow of vodkas flavored in-house or from a menu strong on blinis and caviar, borscht, satsivi chicken, beef stroganoff and smoked fish. If you don't have the time to visit the rowdy Russian enclave in Brighton Beach, Brooklyn, the Russian Samovar is a fine alternative. Many of the diners and drinkers engage in gesticulatory repartee with the owner, Roman Kaplan. One former regular was the poet Joseph Brodsky and in his honor poetry readings take place at the restaurant on Tuesday nights.

Tod Williams's and Billie Tsien's beautifully considered new home for the American Folk Art Museum on West 53rd Street raises the ante for the 2005 opening of Yoshio Taniguchi's expanded Museum of Modern Art on the same block. The architects' solution for the interior combines monumentality and intimacy in perfect proportion. The museum has opened to much critical acclaim: architectural commentator Paul Goldberger has likened it to Sir John Soane's Museum in London for its "truly original spatial exercises within the townhouse volume." The museum's exhibitions are equal in stature to their housing – a recent breakthrough show was a retrospective of self-taught outsider artist Henry Darger. The range of decorative, functional and ceremonial folk art to be found on display includes pottery, trade signs, quilts and wind-up toys.

ROOM WITH A VIEW

24 Rainbow Grill
30 Rockefeller Plaza

When the Rockefeller Center was built in 1934, its superlative flourish was the Rainbow Room on the 65th floor of the tallest and most prominent building in the complex. Its chandeliered circular ballroom has seen three-quarters of a century of dance moves played out across its floor. Today the Room is available for private events only and so you must content yourself with a drink or an expensive meal at the Rainbow Grill. You are paying for the view, so arrive an hour before sundown in time to see the Empire State Building and all the buildings of southern Manhattan glow orange. The men get the added bonus of a great outlook to the north across Central Park from the window of their restroom.

SENSURBOUND CINEMA

25 Ziegfeld Theater
141 West 54th Street

This fabulous movie theater sits on the site of the original "Ziegfeld Follies." Its massive screen, elegant red décor and impeccable sound and projection quality make it the perfect venue for the kinds of big-action epics where you want to share your gasps and tears with 1,200 others.

PIANO FORTE

26 Steinway & Sons
109 West 57th Street

Steinway & Sons was founded in 1853 by German immigrant Henry Engelhard Steinway in a loft on Varick Street. The first piano produced by the company, number 483, was sold to a New York family for $500 and is now displayed at the Metropolitan Museum of Art. In response to huge demand – thanks to the piano's equivalence to a television set in Victorian times – the Steinway business grew to include a factory town in Astoria, Queens, and a 2,000-seat concert hall on 14th Street. The remaining bastion of the piano-maker's empire is a showroom on 57th Street designed in the mid-1920s in a neo-Classical style by Grand Central Station's architects, Warren and Wetmore. Behind the two-story rotunda you will find a stunning display, several soundproofed rooms deep, of every kind of grand, baby grand and upright in every finish imaginable.

QUIETLY ECLECTIC

27 City Club Hotel
124

MIDTOWN ARTIST'S LOFT

28 Chambers Hotel
130

THEATRICAL DINING

29 Town
142

JAPANESE DEPARTMENT STORE

30 Takashimaya
693 Fifth Avenue

From lacquered soup bowls to green seaweed flakes to monochromatic flower arrangements, this Japanese department store, hailing from Osaka, provides seven floors of accoutrements for recreating a perfectly imperfect wabi-sabi lifestyle. The initial design for the store followed the Japanese department-store tradition, which designates the first two floors as gallery space. The 1997 renovation, however, called for 3,000 square feet (270 square meters) of the gallery space to be given over to luggage and travel accessories. The designers at S. Russell Groves managed to continue the gallery theme by using an open grid system of ebonized ash shelves and low tables to display the larger luggage and museum-like stained MDF vitrines lined with Hunan silk for the smaller articles, such as watches and eyewear. The top floor is devoted to high-end hair and beauty products such as Shu Uemura's clear-plastic-packaged make-up, and the basement reveals the restful Tea Box café where you are reminded why it is you are here and not at Macy's.

HOTEL-BAR OPULENCE

31 Oak Bar
The Plaza Hotel, 768 Fifth Avenue

In 1907 Henry Janeway Hardenbergh, who also designed the Dakota apartments, provided his clients with a French chateau of a hotel on the southern edge of Central Park. The Oak Bar, on its ground floor, is a classic hotel bar that befits its opulent setting. Cigars and port are the requisite accessories in this clubhouse interior with its 24-foot (7-meter) ceilings, sable oak walls with fluted columns and 100-year-old murals by Everett Shin. During the 1920s F. Scott Fitzgerald and Ernest Hemingway held court beneath the Oak Bar's hand-carved pilasters and it wasn't until 1974 that women were permitted to share in its Old-World enchantment. Today, its convenient location, at the top of Fifth Avenue's department store-rich strip, is conducive to a hot toddy or aperitif after a hard day's shopping.

STEINWAY & SONS

Upper East Side
Upper West Side
Harlem

HARLEM

EAST
HARLEM

West 127th Street
West 126th Street

East 127th Street
East 126th Street

West 125th Street

East 125th Street

Triborough Bridge

West 125th Street

Studio
Museum

Marcus
Garvey
Park

MORNINGSIDE
HEIGHTS

West 116th Street

East 116th Street

Morningside
Park

Cathedral Parkway

Central Park North

East 106th Street

West 106th Street

Conservatory
Garden

MANHATTAN
VALLEY

SPANISH
HARLEM

97th Street Traverse Road

West 96th Street

East 96th Street

Reservoir

UPPER
WEST
SIDE

Cooper Hewitt

East 91st Street
East 90th Street
East 89th Street
East 88th Street

Guggenheim

86th street Traverse Road

West 86th Street

East 86th Street

Neue Galerie

West 84th Street

Central Park

UPPER
EAST
SIDE

West 83rd Street

Metropolitan
Museum of Art

West 82nd Street
West 81st Street

Belvedere
Lake

West 80th Street

Museum of
Natural
History

79th Street Traverse Road

East 79th Street

West 79th Street

West 77th St.

East 77th Street
East 76th Street

The Lake

East 72nd Street

West 72nd Street

West 70th St.

Frick
Collection

Asia
Society

East 71st St.
East 70th St.

West 67th St.

65th Street Traverse Road

East 67th St.
East 66th St.

West 66th St.

Central
Park
Zoo

Julliard

West 65th St.

Lincoln
Center

Adams
House

West 62nd St.

East 63rd St.
East 62nd St.
East 61st St.
East 60th St.

West 60th St.

The
Pond

Columbus
circle

Central Park South

East 59th St.
East 58th St.

Queensboro Bridge

West 58th St.

East 57th Street

West 57th Street

Approximate scale

1 kilometer

1/2 mile

The Upper East Side is one of the city's most enduring prestigious neighborhoods. Its zip code, 10021, is the wealthiest in the nation and explains the concentration of classy boutiques and European patisseries on Madison Avenue. The original owners of the Fifth and Park Avenue mansions, families such as the Whitneys, the Astors, the Straights, the Dillons, the Dukes, the Mellons and the Pulitzers, all moved here from downtown in the late 1800s once Central Park was opened. Today many of these grand homes house the city's most venerable museums.

The Upper West Side has its own museums such as the American Museum of Natural History with its newly added Rose Center for Earth and Space, an enormous white sphere suspended in a glass and wire cube. Its residents are stereotypically thought of as intellectually and politically liberal. The UWS is also known for its grand apartment buildings such as the Art Déco–style San Remo, with its ornate twin towers concealing water tanks, and the Dakota on the west edge of the park at 72nd Street, which is, at 120 years old, a grandfather of a New York luxury apartment. The Dakota (named as a joke at the time of its building in 1884 for its "far western" location) is a sought-after address, despite its notoriety as the location for the disturbing movie *Rosemary's Baby* and the place where resident John Lennon was shot. Strawberry Fields, Yoko Ono's memorial to the Beatle, landscaped by Bruce Kelly in 1983, is just a little way into the park outside the Dakota.

The area of Manhattan north of Central Park was covered with wooded hills and valleys and inhabited by Indians when the Dutch started the settlement of Nieuw Haarlem in 1658. A late-19th-century building boom, stimulated by the extension of subways to the north of the island, went bust and African–Americans who had been pushed out of other areas began to rent the empty apartment buildings. By the 1910s Harlem had become the biggest black community in the United States and all through the 1920s and 1930s blacks streamed in from the southern states to feed a black cultural explosion known as the Harlem Renaissance. The Sugar Cane Club and Cotton Club hosted Count Basie, Duke Ellington and countless others. Lena Horne got her start here and literary giants Langston Hughes and James Baldwin were native sons. Today, although Harlem's historic liberators and orators are written into its streets and institutions and even though a handful of jazz clubs still survive, the neighborhood is mostly forward-looking. Violent crime, which had plagued its streets, has been significantly reduced and in 2001 former President Bill Clinton moved his office to 55 West 125th Street, just two factors in a widespread revitalization that makes Harlem the neighborhood to watch.

RALPH LAUREN

Matthew Kenney's newest restaurant takes his "C" theme to new uptown heights. The previous two downtown sisters are Canteen and Commune. Commissary has a sleek setting created by David Schefer Design using wraparound windows, black-stained floors and a polished white circular bar for dramatic emphasis. Pistachio-and-anise-crusted halibut, roasted cod glazed with vinegar and Riesling and tender venison chops paired with a juniper-and-celery-root gratin are just some of the Italian- and Asian-influenced dishes on Kenney's modern American menu. The bar area beneath the custom-designed chandelier is a great place to join flirty-somethings for an after-shopping martini.

This lavish mansion, the former home of the steel and railway tycoon Henry Clay Frick, houses a remarkable collection of paintings by all the weighty European masters. The intimate size of the museum, set back from Fifth Avenue by an elevated garden and a tranquil interior court planted with exotic palms, orchids and ferns and centered on an enormous fountain, make the Frick one of New York's most manageable and memorable museum experiences. Holbein's *Sir Thomas More*, Bellini's *St. Francis in the Desert* and Ingres's *The Comtesse d'Hausonville* are just some of the treasures to behold in its four sumptuous rooms. Take a moment to look through the cast-iron gate from East 70th Street at the garden designed in 1977 by Russell Page. And, if you have time, wander up the leafy block towards the Asia Society for a tasting menu of architectural styles. The elegant houses that line this street range from an 1863 white-painted brownstone at no. 129 to an International Style edifice at no. 124, designed in 1940 by William Lescaze.

Bartholomew Voorsanger is the architect of the recently reconfigured Asia Society on the corner of a leafy block of East 70th Street. He opened up the building's lobby and enclosed it partially in glass, then connected the building's four public floors with a free-floating staircase with white steel supports, blue laminated glass steps and light birch rails. The permanent gallery displays Korean ceramics, Indian miniatures, Japanese Buddhist paintings, Indonesian textiles and Thai sculptures and the temporary exhibitions focus on various themes in pan-Asian culture. Be sure to stop awhile in the skylit Garden Court Café.

The Rhinelander mansion building in which the Lauren fantasy world of WASPY privilege unfolds was originally designed in the 1890s by Kimball & Thompson. The 1980s renovation saved antique fixtures and original mouldings. To amplify the aura of a leisure-filled lifestyle of a fictionalized prewar English gentility, the decorators added antique display furniture, Persian carpets, vintage riding boots, Vuitton trunks, cashmere upholstery, camelhair drapes, antique Baccarat chandeliers and Lalique panels.

On the ground floor of the Richard Gluckman–designed New York headquarters of Sotheby's is a restaurant for dealers and collectors who've worked up an appetite on the auction floor. Dineen Nealy Architects have created a space that they describe as "clubby." Its laurel-wood walls showcase a revolving selection of art in a less formal context than that provided by the offices and galleries on the upper floors. The restaurant exudes an atmosphere of comfort, thanks in part to the muted color scheme and the use of soft materials, such as calfskin and chenille upholstery. The culinary emphasis is on contemporary American seasonal fare, and the prix-fixe menu might include braised lobster with corn relish, sautéed quail with bacon and salsify and grey sole with Manila clams and summer truffles.

8 Cooper-Hewitt, National Design Museum
2 East 91st Street

Cooper–Hewitt National Design Museum sits under the imperial umbrella of the Smithsonian Institution and is the only museum in the United States devoted exclusively to historic and contemporary design. Its collections of 250,000 objects and exhibitions – such as "National Design Triennial: Inside Design Now" – are housed in the former home of industrial magnate Andrew Carnegie. The 64-room mansion, built from 1899 to 1902, is a challenging environment in which to present modern design, but its curators keep trying. The Arthur Ross Terrace and Garden, which is the scene of DJ sessions and many design-related gatherings in the summer, is a bucolic bonus to your visit.

9 Metropolitan Museum of Art
1000 Fifth Avenue

It's beyond huge. It's overwhelming. Even the long-distance runners among art lovers will need to take care to pace themselves in this venerable museum. Many of the Met's departments are extensive enough to be museums in themselves and it is advisable to treat them as such, one day at a time. The American Wing holds one of the most comprehensive collections of American painting and sculpture in the world. In the decorative arts section, seek out the Frank Lloyd Wright living room.

10 Iris and B. Gerald Cantor Roof Garden
Metropolitan Museum of Art, 1000 Fifth Avenue

If you do nothing else, and providing it is some time between the month of May and late fall, you should ascend to the Iris and B. Gerald Cantor Roof Garden where, every year, a new sculpture show is installed. You can enjoy a sandwich and a drink and look over the treetops of Central Park as the sun dips behind them. A glorious finale to a day of art appreciation.

11 Seventh Regiment Armory
640 Park Avenue

The venue for numerous art and antique fairs, this fantastical French medieval-style fortress is a treasure in itself. The Tiffany Room, encrusted with decorative stained glass, mosaic and metalwork, is the only existing example of Louis Comfort Tiffany's lavish interior design in the city. Upstairs is the Seventh Regiment Mess and Lounge, a faded 1950s time capsule of a restaurant.

12 Ursus Rare Books
Mezzanine of Carlyle Hotel, 981 Madison Avenue

A comprehensive selection of art reference books, superb copies of rare books in all fields and antique decorative prints can be found and browsed in this well-established store on the mezzanine of the Carlyle Hotel. Peter Kraus's collection is particularly strong in the areas of art, architecture, literature, travel and illustrated children's books. You might find a copy of *Alice in Wonderland* signed by Alice Liddell or a first edition of Ludwig Bemelmans's *Madeline* to put you in the mood for the author and artist's namesake bar downstairs.

13 Bemelmans Bar
Carlyle Hotel, 35 East 76th Street

The walls of this dimly lit piano bar were painted by Ludwig Bemelmans, a 1940s Carlyle resident. The characters from his famous *Madeline* books are depicted in seasonal Central Park settings and their whimsical charm provides a soothing backdrop for various sequestered celebrities and their afternoon cocktails.

14 The Roosevelt Island Tramway
59th Street and Second Avenue
Guastavino's
409 East 59th Street

For one of the most spectacular views of New York – and at the mere price of a subway token – take a return trip on the Roosevelt Island Tramway. Built by the Swiss company Vonroll under designers Prentice & Chan and Ohlhausen, the aerial tramway has been used since 1976 to shuttle Roosevelt Island residents to and from Manhattan. During the four-minute ride, you are quietly whisked 250 feet (75 meters) above the East River, from where you can gaze up and down the water and along the high-rise canyons of midtown. On your return you'll find sustenance in the monumental vaulted space beneath the Queensboro Bridge. Guastavino, British design guru Terence Conran's stylish restaurant, was created in collaboration with Hardy Holzman Pfeiffer Associates, who meticulously restored the ribbed-tile vaulting by Rafael Guastavino y Esposito.

15 Neue Galerie
1048 Fifth Avenue

The collection of this small museum is dedicated to early-20th-century German and Austrian art. The original landmark building is a very fine mansion, dating from 1914, but it is the exquisitely restrained interior restoration at the hands of Annabelle Selldorf that will bring your applause. The paintings, sculptures and art objects stand out dramatically against Selldorf's quiet yet luminous environments. She has also isolated the major architectural features of the building, designed by Carrère and Hastings, so the spiraling marble and wrought-iron stair, the domed skylight and the marble and wood wainscoting can be appreciated.

VIENNESE PASTRIES
16 Café Sabarsky
Neue Galerie, 1048 Fifth Avenue

Café Sabarsky is the museum's excellent eatery, operated by Kurt Gutenbrunner, chef and owner of the acclaimed restaurant Wallsé. With its black-and-white tiled floor, lighting fixtures by Josef Hoffman, furniture by Adolf Loos and banquettes upholstered in an Otto Wagner fabric, Sabarsky draws inspiration from the Viennese cafés that were the centers of intellectual and artistic activity in the early 20th century. The menu focuses on traditional Austrian dishes and does not omit specialties such as strudel and Linzertorte.

ICON OF MODERN MUSEUMS
17 Solomon R. Guggenheim Museum
1071 Fifth Avenue

Set amid the restrained and opulent apartment buildings that line Central Park's eastern side, Frank Lloyd Wright's fantastic white spiraling edifice edges into view as you walk up Fifth Avenue. Opened in 1959 to considerable excitement and controversy, the museum represents the highpoint of America's best-known modern architect. And if the building itself weren't enough reason to visit, the collection is outstanding. Coiling your way down from the top, you will encounter Peggy Guggenheim's trove of Cubist, Surrealist and Abstract Expressionist works and the outstanding photography collection that holds more than 200 Robert Mapplethorpes. You will end up in the atrium below, where an impressive Friday-night music program, often tied to the current exhibition, takes place.

SECRET GARDEN
18 Conservatory Gardens, Central Park
Fifth Avenue and 105th Street

Central Park divides the two "Uppers," which tend to feel like estranged sisters. The people who live in these neighborhoods are fiercely loyal to their locale, so it is not uncommon to find people who have not gone to the "other side" for decades. The park itself is a design masterpiece. "Every foot of the park's surface, every tree and bush, as well as every arch, roadway and walk, has been placed where it is with a purpose," said its landscape architect, Frederick Law Olmsted. When, in 1857, the park began to be transformed from a dump and a bone-boiling plant into an urban idyll, it was surrounded only by open country and squatter shacks. The park's fringes were quickly developed, the biggest surge taking place between 1900 and 1920. Most of these buildings exhibit neo-Georgian, neo-Federal, neo-French or neo-Italian Renaissance styling. Aid your cultural digestion with a stroll through the symmetrical walks of the three formal gardens that constitute the Conservatory Gardens. These gardens – English, Italian and French – were added to Central Park's evolving grand plan in the 1930s, replacing the mouldering greenhouses established by the park's first gardener, Ignaz Pilat. Six acres (2.5 hectares) of hedges, canopied crab-apple trees, beautifully manicured lawns, a trellis of wisteria, profusions of flowers, fountains and more await you in this seldom-visited corner of the park.

RESTORED TO LIFE
19 72nd Street Subway
At Broadway

Make your entrance to the Upper West Side via this Flemish Renaissance–style subway station control house, which occupies its own island at 72nd Street and Broadway. Designed in 1904 by Heins & Lafarge, it has just been restored using the same materials as the original.

NATURAL HISTORY FOR THE HOME
20 Maxilla and Mandible
451 Columbus Avenue

Just one block north of the American Museum of Natural History is a showroom where you can actually take the natural history exhibits home. Specimens from around the world, including bones and skeletons, fossils, eggs, insects, seashells and the supplies necessary to their display can be found in this emporium of anatomical, paleontological, osteological and entomological oddities.

FOODIES' BAZAAR
21 Zabar's
2245 Broadway

Even though you'll want to stop still and gaze around at the crazy interior of this New York institution, you'll be moved on by the sharp elbows of primarily Jewish shoppers focused intently on their purchases of hand-sliced nova, rye bread, challah and chicken pot pie. The smells of cheese, fresh bagels and ground coffee pull you up and down the aisles, on the shelves of which imported packages of dried fruits and biscuits teeter perilously. This food bazaar gives you a real taste of New York.

SMOKED FISH AND HISTORY
22 Barney Greengrass Sturgeon King
136

HISTORIC BOHEMIAN HAUNT
23 Café des Artistes
1 West 67th Street

For a perfect drink before a performance at the Lincoln Center, make your way to the hidden wood-paneled bar at the back of this romantic old-world restaurant. The neo-Gothic Hotel des Artistes was designed in 1917 by George Mort Pollard. The studio apartments did not have kitchens but its tenants, although they were all artists, were hardly of the starving variety. They could congregate in the café, wrapped with Howard Chandler Christy's mural of frolicking nude nymphs, for bistro food and conversation or send fresh ingredients to the kitchens via dumb-waiters and receive meals in return. Among the hotel's most famous residents were Isadora Duncan, Noel Coward, Rudolf Valentino and Norman Rockwell.

PRE-OPERA BISTRO
24 Café Luxembourg
200 West 70th Street

The 1980s take on a Déco interior includes a zinc bar, wicker chairs, black-and-white terrazzo floor and dairy wall tiles. The eclectic brasserie menu is perfect for pre-opera grazing. Sit at the bar for some fried oysters and champagne, elbow to elbow with discerning celebrities who weren't up for the trek 90 blocks south to the Odeon.

CULTURAL MEGAPLEX
25 Lincoln Center for the Performing Arts
65th Street at Columbus Avenue

Even if you do not have tickets to see Plácido Domingo in *Andrea Chénier*, it is worth standing for a few moments at the center of this vast performing arts complex to soak up the urban scene. Bejeweled music- and ballet-lovers crisscross the plaza or wait for their dates on the edge of the central fountain. A variety of performance spaces were built in the late 1950s and 1960s by the stars of the day, such as Philip Johnson (state theater), Eero Saarinen (repertory theater) and Max Abramovitz (philharmonic hall). The Metropolitan Opera House, designed by Wallace K. Harrison in 1966 and featuring enormous Marc Chagall paintings, is a spectacular venue in which to see a Met production under the artistic direction of James Levine.

UPMARKET AMERICAN BRASSERIE
26 Ouest
2315 Broadway

This New American bistro uses tall-sided padded circular booths to create intimate cocoons in a dining place of dramatic scale. Chef-owner Tom Valenti's acclaimed menu offers such dishes as house-smoked sturgeon with frisée, lardons and a poached egg that reference the smoked-fish-and-bagels neighborhood's heritage. For the entrées, however, it leans on bold preparations of meat and poultry.

FOOD FOR THE SOUL
27 Sylvia's Soul Food Restaurant
328 Lenox Avenue (Malcolm X Boulevard)

For hot ribs, coconut cake and some Southern comfort, pop
into Sylvia's joint. Sylvia and Herbert Woods met in a
South Carolina bean field when they were 11 and 12 years
old, respectively. They married in 1943 and set up their
soul food restaurant in 1962. The restaurant has expanded
from an original capacity of 35 to fill almost an entire
block, but it remains a wholly African–America-owned and
-run business. Try the gospel lunch after Sunday services
at the Abyssinian Baptist Church.

GOSPEL CHURCH
28 Abyssinian Baptist Church
132 Odell Clark Place

Built in 1923 by Charles W. Bolton, this blue-stone neo-
Gothic church is renowned for its late pastor, Adam
Clayton Powell, Jr., the first black congressman from
New York City. Services are at 9:00 a.m. and 11:00 a.m.
on Sundays.

HARLEM JAZZ DEN
29 Lenox Lounge
288 Lenox Avenue (Malcolm X Boulevard)

This legendary lounge, specifically the Zebra room, has
played host to Billie Holiday, Miles Davis and John
Coltrane, among others. The original Art Déco interior with
zebra-striped walls, tiled floor and padded leather ceiling
has been restored, but the history of Harlem's premier jazz
venue (now that the Cotton Club and the Savoy Ballroom
have gone) still hangs in the air like smoke.

AFRICAN-AMERICAN ARTS
30 The Studio Museum in Harlem
144 West 125th Street

The museum's unique focus on African–American art
and that of the African Diaspora has produced some
groundbreaking exhibitions under the curatorial guidance
of exhibition director, Thelma Golden. Central to the
museum's mission is the challenging of canonical histories
of European and American Modernism. The vibrant
artists-in-residence program produces regular showings
of emerging artists who work in the studio areas of
the building. For lunch at Sylvia's you need only cross
the street.

Williamsburg
Long Island City

With what, to locals, seems like improbable velocity, the Brooklyn neighborhood of Williamsburg has in a few short years transformed itself from a declining industrial district to an artists' enclave and a hipster destination spot. In the mid-1800s Williamsburg was a fashionable resort area, with hotels, clubs and beer gardens that gathered around the Brooklyn ferry park attracting industrialists and professionals. Once the Williamsburg Bridge was opened, it became increasingly industrialized. Henry Miller remembered "the ironworks where the red furnace glowed and men walked toward the glowing pit with huge shovels in their hands" of the 1890s Williamsburg that he grew up in. At that time the waterfront was cluttered with docks, shipyards, warehouses, distilleries, taverns, mills, metal works and breweries. Today there are fewer than 9,000 manufacturing jobs (compared to 93,000 in 1961). Fortunately, there are still enough broccoli-packing factories, sugar refineries and an eclectic ethnic mix of Puerto Ricans, Poles and Hasidim to prevent the burgeoning scene from becoming too homogeneous, so far remaining relatively untouched by the invasion of global franchises. Thanks to its idiosyncratic shops and relaxed attitude, on weekday afternoons it has a quiet, almost villagelike, atmosphere. But already many of the artists who forged the way in the early 1990s for the flood of galleries have been priced out of the lofts they once squatted. As these artists move further south and east, so new bars and restaurants follow in their wake.

As yet there is no hotel in the neighborhood, so stay in Manhattan and take the L train three stops from Union Square. Bedford Avenue, the main drag, and the streets between North 9th and Broadway that cross it, are dotted with enough boutiques, antique shops, galleries, cafés, restaurants and bars to keep you happily occupied for an afternoon that may well turn into night.

Long Island City, several miles to the north of Williamsburg, is another wind-swept industrial zone, with some residential pockets of Asian and Latin American immigrants, that is undergoing an exciting revitalization thanks to a growing art, film and design community. Either take the G train north towards Queens or return to Manhattan and pick up the Queens Art Link, a shuttle bus that departs from West 53rd Street between Fifth and Sixth Avenues for the art destinations MoMA QNS, P.S.1, the Socrates Sculpture Park and the Isamu Noguchi Museum. New York seems to have fixed its greedy gaze on Long Island City in the sprawling borough of Queens that has, until now, remained a frontier to most Manhattanites. The advanced guard has already installed itself in choice lofts, and it may not be long before Long Island City, just like Williamsburg, has its corner bodegas turned into cappuccino-serving cafés playing electronica.

FARM-GROWN PRODUCE

1 Greenmarket

Union Square, East 17th Street and Broadway

An integral part of the Williamsburg experience is a ride on the L train. Its cars are crowded with self-expression until the small hours of the morning and the ride from Union Square to Bedford Avenue is always visually stimulating. If it is a Monday, Wednesday, Friday or Saturday, before you duck underground to the station, you can savor the smells and colors of the farm-grown produce stalls that cluster at the northern end of Union Square. The Square, dating from 1839, is a traditional platform for political rallies and labor protests. The few remaining radicals now share the steps and railings with skateboarding tricksters.

LOCAL COLOR

2 Pete's Candy Store

709 Lorimer Street

You will discover the real charm of this old-fashioned bar in a 1900s brick storefront in the narrow, curtained-off back room, which features an upholstered vaudeville stage lit with vanity bulbs. This room, padded like the interior of a jewel box, hosts nightly performances by local bluegrass bands and poets, booked by co-owner Juliana Nash. Bingo and trivia quiz nights on Tuesdays and Wednesdays are wildly popular with the vintage T-shirt set.

HIGH FASHION IN THE 'BURG

3 ISA

163

DINER STYLE

4 Diner

138

CARNIVORES' CHOICE

5 Peter Luger's Steakhouse

139

MOROCCAN-MOSAIC RESTAURANT

6 Oznot's Dish

79 Berry Street

There are two times of the day when this Moroccan-infused restaurant shines brightest. One is the brunching hour that stretches between noon and 3 p.m. and involves unusual takes on breakfast fare such as cardamom French toast with raisins, nutmeg, yogurt and fresh fruit or poached eggs wrapped in cured salmon on corn frittatas. You'll sit with families and gallery-goers on mismatched chairs in the main room or in the sunny, greenhouselike lean-to at the back of the restaurant. The other is at twilight, when you can perch at the mosaic-encrusted bar and sample from the extensive wine list.

EMERGING TENDENCIES

7 Momenta Art

72 Berry Street

Momenta Art is a not-for-profit exhibition space directed by the artist Eric Heist. Its two-person shows, with a bias toward American artists, and its thematic exhibits such as "Pop Patriotism," curated in response to the national surge of flagwaving after 9/11, are consistently thought-provoking. For each exhibition in this pristine white box of a space, the gallery publishes a newsletter that includes information about the artists and their works.

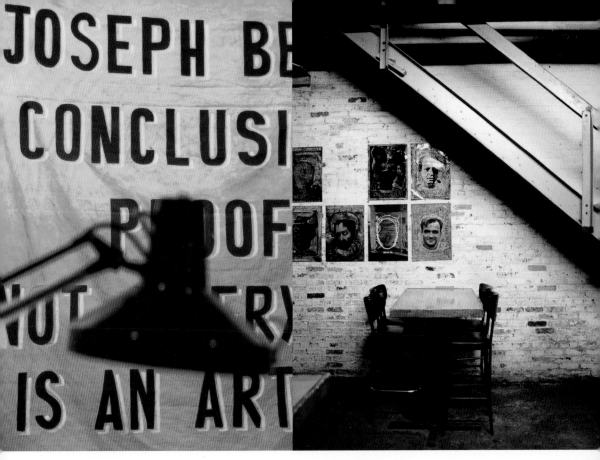

8 Pierogi 2000
177 North 9th Street

The name of this gallery, one of the most established in the neighborhood, is a reference to the dumpling favored by the vicinity's Polish residents. Pierogi 2000 has monthly shows featuring the work of artists from Williamsburg, Brooklyn and beyond. You can riffle through samples of work from more than 500 mostly American artists, as long as you don the white gloves provided. The original unframed works stored in flatfiles are affordable and include the work of such notables as Lawrence Weiner, Keith Tyson and Bob and Roberta Smith.

WILLIAMSBURG'S ART BAR
9 Galapagos
70 North 6th Street

You enter this bar and performance space, barely signaled from the street by a red light, via a metal walkway that bridges an oily dark reflecting pool. The converted mayonnaise factory is the venue for Monday evening burlesque shows in the candlelit bar area and a myriad of experimental performances, underground film screenings, album launch parties and book readings in the garagelike back space.

INDEPENDENT BOOKSTORE
10 Spoonbill & Sugartown
218 Bedford Avenue

Located in the Realform Girdle Building smack in the center of Williamsburg's thoroughfare of cool, Bedford Avenue, this wonderful bookshop restores your confidence in the possibility that a huge, mass-market company will not preemptively strike the whole of the bookselling trade. Specializing in used, rare and new books on contemporary art, art history, architecture and design, the store numbers among its staff some large sleepy cats that drape themselves over the piles of volumes waiting to be shelved.

DINER CAR
11 Relish
225 Wythe Avenue

A location scout's fantasy, this silver diner with original fittings and its idyllic patio is one of Williamsburgers' favorite hangouts. The food is comfort-oriented, exemplified by classics such as cheeseburgers and jumbo "tobacco" onion rings coated in cinnamon and cayenne spice batter. The self-consciously cool waiting staff play their own mix CDs and bestow their slight attention on your dining needs when it suits them.

CLUB ROCK
12 Luxx
256 Grand Street

The unofficial headquarters of the Electroclash revolution and the initiator of the hedonistic gay night, "Berliniamsburg," this lurid rock club owned by Larry Tee has attracted a devoted following of 30-something club kids. Reflective wallpaper and a high-tech sound system add a dose of glamor to the rock provided by local and national underground bands.

BIKERS' BAR
13 Moto
394 Broadway

A recent addition to the area's casually hip bar scene is Moto. Motorbike enthusiasts Billy Phelps and John McCormick converted a decrepit check-cashing joint into a motorcycle-themed no-frills bar with a menu of snacking food. Situated in south Williamsburg, where a Hassidic Jewish community meets a Puerto Rican one, the bar prefigures the imminent southward development of the Williamsburg neighborhood.

ART GOES BACK TO SCHOOL
14 P.S.1 Contemporary Art Center
22–25 Jackson Avenue

The corridors and classrooms of the converted Public School No. 1 now reverberate to the sound of the Prada heels of contemporary art lovers. Be sure to seek out the James Turrell Room at dusk for a sublime encounter with a square-shaped patch of shifting sky. And for the non-claustrophobes, find Robert Wogan's installation on the fourth floor, in which you enter a pitch-black passageway that narrows and finally ejects you into a pyramid-shaped room showing a video of the pre-renovated P.S.1. Each year the courtyard area is transformed into an urban playground by an emerging architect – Bill Massie, Linda Roy and SHoP are among the past contributors. The installation, usually water-themed, becomes the hopping scene of Saturday afternoon DJ Warm Up Sessions.

MODERN ART'S URBAN SAFARI
15 MoMA QNS
4520 33rd Street

The modern art museum's new temporary quarters are in the former Swingline staple factory in Long Island City, Queens. Architect Michael Maltzan has designed the building to be seen from the elevated (No. 7 line) train. Maltzan, along with the graphic-design firms Base and 212 Associates, applied panels to the building's roof, each containing a piece of one of the letters of the MoMA logo, so that the name of this modern art behemoth materializes progressively. The galleries are understated and do little to mask the building's industrial character. The original location on West 53rd Street, currently being renovated and enlarged to the design of Japanese architect Yoshio Taniguchi, will reopen in 2005.

SCULPTED TRANQUILITY
16 Isamu Noguchi Garden Museum
32–37 Vernon Boulevard

Thirteen indoor and outdoor galleries within a converted factory building encircle a tranquil garden containing Noguchi's major granite and basalt sculptures. The factory was the office, studio and storage facility of the Japanese sculptor and designer of furniture, stage sets and public spaces. On exhibition are more than 240 of Noguchi's works, including stone, metal, wood and clay sculptures, models for public projects and gardens and dance sets. His Akari light sculptures are for sale in the museum store–café, enabling you to take a piece of Zen home with you.

The museum is currently housed in a temporary location (36-01 43rd Avenue, Long Island City), so be sure to check which location is being used at the time of your visit.

ART BY THE RIVER
17 Socrates Sculpture Park
Broadway and Vernon Boulevard

Set on the Long Island City bank of the East River with midtown high-rises as a backdrop, this outdoor sculpture park is the site of large-scale works by both emerging and recognized artists. Socrates Sculpture Park was an abandoned riverside landfill and illegal dumpsite until 1986 when a coalition of artists and community members, under the leadership of artist Mark di Suvero, transformed it into an open studio and exhibition space and a neighborhood park for local residents. Exhibitions rotate on a semi-annual basis; a visit to Socrates a month or two preceding an opening allows one to see the sculpture-making process.

P.S.1.

THE INSTITUTE FOR CONTEMPORARY ART

ART

Park Slope
Smith Street
Fort Greene

"No! Sleep! Till Brooklyn!" The Beastie Boys' rallying cry may have made sense in 1990 but today Brooklyn has enough going on to keep you up all night. Several of its neighborhoods — DUMBO, Smith Street, Fort Greene and Red Hook among them — are sprouting new scenes that have earned them multiple stars on New York's style map. The fastest-developing destination territories tend, unsurprisingly, to be clustered near the three bridges that connect Brooklyn to Lower Manhattan.

Park Slope is the older hippy sister of the bunch. If it doesn't already, it should be able to lay claim to having the largest number of baby strollers per block of anywhere in the nation. It's impossible to carry your soy-milk decaffeinated cappuccino more than a few Birkenstock-shod feet without bumping into another set of proud young parents, often same-sex. The charming brownstones and mansions of this district were built around Prospect Park's Manhattan-facing aspect in the late 1800s after it opened its gates and the Brooklyn Bridge was completed.

Brooklyn's most happening scene is acted out on a section of Smith Street that has its head in Boerum Hill — a neighborhood of brownstones with prices kept in check by the proximity of projects — and its tail in Italianate Carroll Gardens. Until the late 1990s, when an urban renewal project paved the way for pioneering restaurants such as Patois, this stretch of Smith was a no-go zone. Now the street, lined with trees and wrought-iron street lamps, is peopled by shoppers and diners a few years older and some degrees less fashion-obsessed than those found on its rival, Williamsburg's Bedford Avenue. By day you can browse the vintage and contemporary clothes stores as well as the two furniture stores that double as cafés. In the evening you can dine on bistro fare, at Café LuluC or Bar Tabac, or on more sophisticated cuisine at Grocery. Drinking venues range from nicotine-stained classics, such as The Brooklyn Inn, to the contemporary good looks of BarBelow.

The popular image of Fort Greene is one colored by Spike Lee's famously bittersweet portrayals of the artsy, well-educated African-American district in which he came of age. And while the historic district of Fort Greene — with its luscious late-19th-century brownstones that line the streets to the south and east of Fort Greene Park, named for its pivotal role in the Revolutionary War — is still characterized by the racial and economic diversity that Lee documented, the nightlife around Lafayette and DeKalb Avenues is an utterly contemporary phenomenon. French bistros such as Loulou, Chez Oscar, A Table and Liquors cater for the Brooklyn Academy of Music (BAM) crowds and an ever-increasing local population of young professionals, reaping the benefits of an area rich in black culture.

PARKLIFE
1 Bed and Breakfast on the Park

116

DEMENTED ASSEMBLAGE
2 McSweeney's Store

166

HORTICULTURAL TREASURE
3 Brooklyn Botanic Garden
1000 Washington Avenue

Known for its annual Cherry Blossom Festival, the Brooklyn Botanic Garden is among the best-regarded and most needed in the country. Stroll beneath wisteria-laden trellises to the rose garden boasting 1,200 different varieties. The recently restored Japanese garden features an authentic teahouse that overlooks a pond seething with turtles and giant koi. A great blue heron, a frequent visitor to the pond, completes the tranquil scene. The greenhouses contain one of the world's largest collections of bonsai trees, some well over 100 years old. Founded in 1910, the Brooklyn Botanic Garden has far more charm than its larger counterpart in the Bronx.

ART AT THE PARK
4 Brooklyn Museum of Art
200 Eastern Parkway

The Brooklyn Museum of Art is the second largest art museum in New York City and one of the largest in the United States. Although its fame stems largely from controversy kindled by ex-Mayor Giuliani who withdrew public funding for the Museum's staging of the "Sensation" exhibition, back in 1999, its permanent collection is a cultural force to be reckoned with. The collection includes more than one and a half million objects, from ancient Egyptian masterpieces to contemporary art. The façade of the museum's Beaux Arts structure, designed in the late 19th century by McKim, Mead & White, has just undergone a major renovation and restructuring by Polshek Partnership Architects, which adds a new entrance pavilion. A varied program of music and entertainment takes place on the first Saturday of each month.

MYTHICAL MERCHANDISE
5 Castor & Pollux

174

BURNISHED BAR
6 Brooklyn Inn
148 Hoyt Street

A classic old-time Brooklyn establishment dating from 1868, the inn features a large, ornate antique bar, huge mirrors and high tin ceiling. During the day, light streams in through the dusty windows falling on the open notebooks and discarded pens of the hard-drinking regulars who seem to include a disproportionate number of writers. Argue about Kierkegaard or play a neighborly game of pool in the back room. At night, the place can fill up with young professionals back from a hard day in "the city." With only a neon "Pilsner Urquell" sign on its Gothic iron-and-wood exterior, you'll need to follow the locals and their dogs to find this corner spot.

WINE AND CHEESE
7 Sherwood Café at Robin des Bois

153

LAID-BACK BEATS CAFÉ
8 Halcyon
227 Smith Street

A starry line-up of up-and-coming DJs drop beats nightly at this multifunctional space that combines the features of bar, café and record and vintage housewares store. The sound system is designed by David Soto and the furniture, all of which is for sale, is mid-century modern. The drinks list is limited – beer, wine and coffee are the staples – but the music and its aficionados, with their headphones and hoods, are the draw.

MARKET FRESH
9 Grocery
288 Smith Street

Thirteen simple paper-topped tables in an unadorned storefront constitute this restaurant, which, with its flavorful seasonal American fare, transcends "neighbor-hood" status. Co-chefs and owners, Charles Kiely and Sharon Pachter, take the time to chat as they bring you your house-made sausage, marinated skirt steak or duck in caramelized wine sauce. Fresh market produce, good meat and fish are the foundation stones of Grocery's cuisine. On summer nights you can sit out back beneath a spreading fig tree in the ivy-walled garden.

WORLD'S BEST CHEESECAKE
10 Junior's
386 Flatbush Avenue

From the day Harry Rosen opened Junior's on Flatbush Avenue in 1950, three generations of his family have been baking "the world's most fabulous cheesecakes" and mixing egg creams for locals and those who venture across the Manhattan Bridge. The vast menu features a mixture of kosher deli, soul food and plain old diner fare. The flashing lights of its signage are particularly photogenic.

THE SOUL OF JAZZ
11 Frank's Lounge
660 Fulton Street

Although Frank's now hosts Bang the Party, a popular event upstairs on alternating Friday nights, for the rest of the time it is mostly locals. Black men wearing three-piece suits and fedoras lean against the bar while their "ladies" sit at the tables. Any single aspect of the bar, taken alone, would be uninspired: shabby carpet, low ceiling and dark paneling. But to go to Frank's on a Thursday when Lonnie Youngblood is blowing his saxophone and the old-timers are holding court is to be transported back in time to a Fort Greene that existed before Spike Lee and the Notorious B.I.G. and to feel the soul behind what would become the hip-hop heart of New York.

PERFORMANCES ON THE EDGE
12 Brooklyn Academy of Music
30 Lafayette Avenue

This recently restored 19th-century building, the cultural cornerstone of Fort Greene as well of the world a very long way beyond it, stages an eclectic mix of opera, dance and experimental performances by the likes of Robert Wilson, Lou Reed, Philip Glass and Laurie Anderson. BAM, as it is universally known, also offers an elegant café for a pre-performance appetizer and drink as well as BAM Rose Cinemas, arguably the best movie theater in the city. Apart from the regular seasonal performances, BAM hosts several festivals, including the feted Next Wave Festival, begun in 1983. Also of note in the immediate vicinity is The Mark Morris Dance Group's brand new studio across the street.

OYSTERS AND CHOPS
13 Gage & Tollner
144

sleep • eat • drink
shop • retreat

sleep

Spectacular lobbies, hip bars and top-notch restaurants, meticulously orchestrated for seeing and being seen in, have become de rigueur in New York's hotels, the enduring legacy of a hotel-design revolution that began in the 1980s. Hoteliers, with Ian Schrager at their vanguard, teamed up with celebrity interior designers to create a relentlessly designed experience that extends from the vase in the bathroom to the matchbooks in the bar. Now that the boutique-hotel look has been copied and diluted around the world, the establishments presented here are singled out for their departures from the formulaic or for their uniqueness, eclecticism or excess.

106 Bed and Breakfast on the Park

1 113 Prospect Park West
Rooms from $250

Prospect Park, Frederick Law Olmsted's and Calvert Vaux's 1873 vision of a bucolic idyll, provides 536 acres (217 hectares) of leafy respite for overtaxed Brooklynites. On its west side, beyond the 90-acre (36-hectare) greensward known as Long Meadow, and at the crown of the slope that runs down through the villagelike neighborhood of Park Slope, is Prospect Park West. The mansions that still grace this avenue were erected in the late 1880s shortly after the completion of the Brooklyn Bridge enabled easier access to Manhattan. Number 113, a four-story brownstone, built in 1892, is one of Brooklyn's top ten landmarks of Victorian architecture. Refashioned in 1987 into a bed and breakfast, it has nine rooms, some with views all the way to the Statue of Liberty and those at the front overlooking the park. Owner Liana Paolella, an antiques dealer as well as innkeeper, has furnished the brownstone with her wares, ranging from the mid-1800s to the early 1900s and including some especially fine oil paintings from her family collection. The original mouldings in the parlor are of intricately carved oak, African mahogany and bird's-eye maple. The suite on the top floor has a double canopy bed swathed in French lace, a large antique bath, a sitting area and a private rooftop garden with views of the city skyline. Breakfast is taken in the Victorian dining room, pooled with colored light from the stained-glass bay windows. A feast consisting of homemade bread, German pancakes, light crêpes, quiche Lorraine and homemade jams and jellies is spread on the huge table, set with Irish linen, Royal Crown Derby and Waterford jars. Rest assured that you will be well fed for your exploration of the linked Brooklyn "villages" of Park Slope, Fort Greene and Boerum Hill.

60 Thompson

60 Thompson Street
Rooms from $200

A treat awaits guests of the 60 Thompson: its rooftop terrace offers a breathtaking panorama of Manhattan's skyline, toothed with water towers in the foreground. The view stretches as far as the Empire State Building to the north and across the Hudson River to New Jersey to the west. The hotel's owners, The Pomeranc Group, had to buy the air rights from all the neighboring buildings for their 13-story hotel to pass local zoning laws. Steve Jacobs, one of the pioneers of the 1980s vogue for SoHo and TriBeCa loft and industrial building conversion, was the architect and Thomas O'Brien, of Aero Studios, the interior designer. O'Brien, whose clients include Giorgio Armani and Ralph Lauren, took his inspiration for this hotel from disparate sources, including the marble floor of a reflecting pool in Pompeii, a 1942 photograph of Burt Lancaster reclining on a long sofa in his Malibu house and the 1930s minimalism of French interior designer Jean-Michel Frank. Visitors approach the hotel, which is between Spring and Broome Streets, and nicely off SoHo's center, through a recessed courtyard planted with white birches. A downstairs entrance foyer introduces the recurring color palette of brown, grey and red and ushers guests upward to the light-filled reception area and to the adjoining bar and lounge on the second floor, scene of many a fashion shoot and celebrity interview. The focus of each guest room is the platform bed that extends from a full-wall leather headboard. The cerused wood furniture includes a sofa, a high-backed Thompson Chair, based on an English Déco chaise O'Brien found in London, and a dark wood table arrangement to replace the traditional hotel desk. The 2,000-square-foot (185-square-meter) duplex penthouse loft with a four-poster king bed and two private garden decks is the hotel's crown jewel.

Gramercy Park Hotel

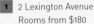 2 Lexington Avenue
Rooms from $180

The Gramercy Park Hotel, a Renaissance Revival–style brick structure, with a two-story stone base topped by balustrade railings, was built in 1927 by Thompson and Churchill. It was once home to 11-year-old President-to-be John F. Kennedy and his parents, Rose and Joseph P. Kennedy. Its roof garden was the setting for the wedding of 27-year-old Humphrey Bogart to Helen Mencken. The hotel overlooks Gramercy Park, a beautiful and very private oasis, for which guests – who have its key for the duration of their stay – and the fireflies that on summer evenings illuminate it in short bursts have to thank developer, Samuel Ruggles. He had the foresight in 1831 to set aside 42 lots in his residential square to ensure "the free circulation of air." The gated park, bounded by landmark buildings, including the Gothic Revival National Arts Club (p. 55) and early-20th-century brownstones, is the core of a particularly fabulous historic district populated by New York's past and current gentry. The hotel's bar, which Babe Ruth was politely asked, on more than one occasion, to leave, emanates shabby gentility and is frequented in equal measure by young media types and silver-haired local residents. In the 1970s it was a renowned rock-star hangout, a fact that did not escape director Cameron Crowe, who used it as a location for his movie *Almost Famous*. The Gramercy has a faded grandeur and an eccentric family ownership that endear it to long-term tenants and returning regulars.

52 **The Inn at Irving Place**

7 56 Irving Place
Rooms from $350

You approach this small, secretive hotel – formed by the joining of two 1830s townhouses – by a flight of steep steps from the sidewalk to the parlor floor. To the left as you enter is Lady Mendl's, an antique-furnished tea salon serving a five-course high tea with sandwiches of the thinly-sliced-cucumber-and-smoked-salmon variety. The dozen atmospheric guest rooms, restored by owner Naomi Blumenthal with Larry Wente in 1994, feature fireplaces (non-usable, unfortunately, but there is a blazing fire in the parlor during winter months) and hardwood floors. They are furnished with period armoires, four-poster brass beds, Oriental rugs and antique lighting fixtures. While some have likened the experience of the Inn to a sojourn with one's eccentric great-aunt, the bed and breakfast has far more romantic potential than such a comparison evokes. The Madame Olenska suite – named for Edith Wharton, who once lived in nearby Gramercy Square – is the largest in the hotel. It boasts a window seat overlooking Irving Place, an antique typewriter and a sitting room in which to take your complimentary continental breakfast and *The New York Times* or to receive your visitors. Every bathroom features an early-20th-century pedestal sink and brass fixtures. And though such luxury might tempt you to stay in your claw-foot tub with a copy of *The Age of Innocence*, observation of more contemporary manners can be found a short walk in any direction from the inn's front door. A few blocks to the southwest is Union Square, originally constructed in 1831 and now home to a bustling Greenmarket (p. 97) above ground and a major subway hub below. Take the L train three stops towards Brooklyn to explore the city's hippest neighborhood and most vibrant emerging art scene, Williamsburg.

The opening of the City Club Hotel signaled the beginning of a new era of what shall henceforth be known as post-boutiquism. Jeff Klein, a worldly socialite and first-time hotelier, dubs his refined travelers' haven an "anti-boutique" with an "anti-lobby" to match. Indeed, in contrast to the wonderland that welcomes guests into the Royalton across the road, this lobby is intentionally small and mousy. With its red coffee table loaded with books and vases of orchids, waxed cork flooring and pillow-strewn window-seat, it reads more like the entrance to a private residence than that of a 65-room hotel in Manhattan's theater district. Interior designer Jeffrey Bilhuber has erred in favor of an eclectic aesthetic. In the mezzanine lounge Queen Anne chairs abut Brancusi stools and a Fabien Baron mylar mobile offsets vintage framed playbills. Bilhuber's blend of traditional and modern sensibilities is played out with impeccable restraint in the guest rooms: The bathrooms are of chocolate-colored marble and nickel chrome, the walls are finished to simulate hand-corrugated plaster, the furniture is Honduran mahogany and the selection of quirky ornaments has been distinctively curated. And, lest one should begin to feel it's all about style, the details add a dose of tangible luxury, such as the television with a mirror screen that dissolves once turned on. All of this adds up to a contemporary version of the comfort once provided by the building's original occupant: a 1904 gentlemen's club.

34 **Hotel Chelsea**

20 222 West 23rd Street
Rooms from $200

Legends of the Chelsea loom even larger than the imposing Victorian–Gothic edifice that dominates much of the block between Seventh and Eighth Avenues on 23rd Street. Apart from the more dramatic scenes that have colored its rooms and corridors, such as Nancy Spungen's stabbing at the hands of boyfriend Sid Vicious in room 100 and Dylan Thomas's last drink in 205, the hotel's guest register is a veritable index of 20th-century American literature. Long-term tenants have included Mark Twain, Tennessee Williams, Arthur Miller and O. Henry; Arthur Clarke penned *2001: A Space Odyssey* and William Burroughs wrote *Naked Lunch* within its walls. But the hotel's location in the gallery district of the city and its residents, including Jim Dine, Claes Oldenburg and Warhol's Chelsea Girls, have earned it the dubious honor of sleeping quarters for the art world – albeit for those with a rock-and-roll- rather than MoMA-inspired interpretation of art. Holly Solomon has a gallery in room 425 and the lobby doubles as a gallery showing the work of previous residents, some of whom purportedly paid for their lodging in kind. Since 2001, a far less down-and-out clientele can be found under the hotel's canopy as they line up for entrance to velvet-roped Serena, a swanky subterranean cocktail bar, named for its owner, a well-known New York caterer. The Chelsea's red-brick façade and lacy wrought-iron balconies are the work of Hubert Pirsson & Co. who built the hotel in 1884 as the city's first co-operative apartment complex. Be warned that seedy cool is apt to teeter dangerously on the edge of downright dingy. But if, like Leonard Cohen, writer of the song "Chelsea Hotel #2," you "love hotels to which, at 4 a.m., you can bring along a midget, a bear and four ladies, drag them to your room and no one cares about it at all," then you'll feel at right at home.

80 **The Lowell**

1 28 East 63rd Street

Rooms from $530

Scandinavian down comforters, Chinese porcelains, 18th-century prints, Fauchon and Dean and Deluca goodies in the minibars and Bulgari amenities in the marble bathrooms – the guest rooms of The Lowell exude uptown luxury from every Frette linen pore. The suites, boasting wood fires, libraries and terraces, are even more sumptuous. Its discreet location on tree-lined East 63rd street in the Upper East Side Historic District and its immaculate service endear this hotel to a privacy-seeking clientele. Originally an apartment hotel of one- and two-bedroom suites, designed in the late 1920s by Henry Stern Churchill, The Lowell is now a landmark building. The exterior of the lower floors features a mosaic façade of brick and glazed terracotta; higher up is a series of asymmetrical terraced setbacks. The gorgeous lobby, designed by Dalmar Tift III, is comprised of Art Déco details, French Empire Style furniture, chiaroscuro walls and a rare desk console signed by Edgar Brandt. The slightly too exquisite chintz of the hotel's furnishings may not suit all tastes, but if you like your country cottages one block from Central Park and within walking distance of all the uptown museums and Madison Avenue boutiques, this will be your whimsical nirvana.

66 | **Chambers Hotel**

28 | 15 West 56th Street
Rooms from $300

Envisioned as an aesthetic juxtaposition of private collector's townhouse and downtown artist's loft, the Chambers Hotel features more than 300 works of contemporary art and, in the rooms, an industrial vernacular of exposed sprinkler pipes, skeletal track lighting, distressed plaster walls and raw, concrete-slab bathroom floors. Twelve artists created wall drawings, paintings and sculptures for the corridors on each of the twelve guest-room floors. Bob and Roberta Smith's installation of witty slogans is painted in vivid hues on the walls of the fourth-floor hallway. The hotel's ingress depends on a spatial sequence to create its dramatic effect: guests enter through oversized black walnut doors, carved in a basket-weave pattern, and are momentarily contained in a small vestibule – as if to intensify the suspense – before they emerge in a soaring, double-height lobby. The 15-story hotel, financed by the owners of the Mercer and designed by David Rockwell, was built from the ground up, an unusual opportunity for this design team since most of the city's boutique hotels are renovations of existing architectural structures. Customized furnishings in the guest rooms include grape- and kiwi-colored felt ottomans and glass desktops on leather-bound sawhorses. The windows are almost floor-to-ceiling and French doors lead to small terraces, made possible by the building's recessed façade. The flooring is wide-plank walnut with area rugs from Tibet and Turkey. Some of the rooms have a hand-tiled soaking tub and all have Bumble and Bumble bath products. For the ultimate touch of midtown-specific opulence, guest phones have a direct-dial line to a Henri Bendel personal shopper who can bring merchandise from the city's most luxurious department store to your room for private perusal.

14 **Tribeca Grand Hotel**

19 2 Sixth Avenue
Rooms from $260

When the Tribeca Grand opened in 2000, the stakes were high. As the younger sibling of the fashion and media industry's digs of choice, the Soho Grand, this new arrival was expected to make its own large statement. The building has a quiet brick façade, with a granite base and cast-iron detailing that nicely echoes the architectural language of the neighborhood but does not seem particularly noteworthy. Only step through the glass doors opened by obliging porters, however, and you see where the Hartz Group and its designer, Larry Bogdanow, decided to put their money. The 10,000-square-foot (930-square-meter), eight-story atrium serves multiple functions – lounge, waiting room, bar, restaurant and meeting place – and it is undoubtedly the spectacular "shouting-piece" of the hotel. Much of the visual drama is achieved by lighting. Focus Lighting's layered illumination plan defines different activity zones by varying light levels and colors while accentuating details and tactile surfaces. A series of 66 paraffin lights flickering against a copper tile-lined niche suggests a "fireplace" at the lobby's north wall. The Church Lounge, as the area at the rear of the lobby is dubbed, is a popular nightlife destination in itself. Guests and visitors lounging on leather sofas and chenille slipper chairs sip cocktails and graze on duck confit baklava, to the beat of guest DJs such as Nickodemus and Zero 7. The 203 smallish guest rooms – stacked on two sides of the triangular-shaped interior and accessed by glass elevators in steel cages – were designed by Calvin Tsao. The emphasis is on ergonomic comfort for the media-dependent business traveler – thoughtful details include Bose Wave CD players, web access via the TV and wireless keyboard, cordless telephones, Herman Miller Aeron desk chairs and bathrooms appointed with Kiehl's potions.

eat

There are some 130 eateries per Manhattan square mile (2.5 square kilometers) that represent every conceivable national and regional cuisine the world has to offer – along with curious fusions of more than one of them – available any time of the day or night. New York is a city that eats out in all variety of manners, two recent trends being reinvigorated interpretations of hotel dining and New American, which celebrates down-home ingredients inventively (sometimes wildly) prepared. Striking décor isn't hard to find, so this selection identifies those places that offer exceptional cuisine or an enduring, often quiet sense of style: places that simply feel good to eat out in.

SMOKED FIS

PRICE PER 1/4 LB

STURGEON	12.00	Whi
Pastrami Salmon or Gravlox	8.75	Whole
Eastern Nova Scotia Salmon	8.75	Center
Western Nova Scotia Salmon	8.25	Jumbo
Belly (Salty) Lox	6.75	Chubs
Kippered (Baked) Salmon	6.75	Rain
able	8.75	Impo

80 **Barney Greengrass Sturgeon King**

22 541 Amsterdam Avenue

This Jewish delicatessen, established at this location in 1927, when the Greengrass family moved their business from Harlem, provides the perfect environment in which to get a smoked-fish taste of Upper West Side life. The interior and the attitude have been cured as perfectly as their specialty sturgeon. The counters burst with three varieties of Russian caviar, smoked rainbow brook trout, pickled herrings, kippered salmon, chopped liver, pastrami and bialys. The atmosphere is old diner, with fluorescent lighting. Faded Formica wainscoting and vinyl are the materials of choice. Upper West Side families, desiccated but immaculately turned-out old timers and writers come here on Saturday mornings for eggs scrambled with nova and onions washed down with cream soda. You'll feel privileged to join them.

NEW STANDARDS
66 **Brasserie**
11 100 East 53rd Street

When the original Brasserie, located in the basement of
Mies van der Rohe's Seagram building, was recently
destroyed by a kitchen fire, experimental architects
Diller + Scofidio were given the opportunity to
redesign the restaurant. With a nod to its heritage –
patrons used to descend perilously steep stairs – the
architects pitched a central glass staircase at a shallow
angle to maximize its intrusion in the middle of the
room. The drama of the diners' sudden appearance
from the reception area is accentuated by the strip of
flat-screen video monitors above the bar that captures
in freeze-frame images of the last 15 people to have
entered the restaurant. A shell of pear wood encases
the dining space, tables are slabs of translucent lime-
cast resin, the chairs are Eero Saarinen's "Executives"
covered in white leather. Chef Luc Dimnet has
constructed a contemporary bistro menu with Brasserie
classics indicated in bold face. For dessert, the Moorish
chocolate beignets are perfect for sharing.

CHIC SUSHI
14 **Bond Street**
62 6 Bond Street

Bond Street's co-owner, Jonathan Morr, says of
restaurant design that, "When you create a space, it's not
about design really. It's not even about taste. It's about
creating a feel." The feel of this nouvelle Japanese
restaurant, shaped by architect Ilan Waisbrod of the firm
Studio Gaia, is refined and subdued, with only the
oversized floral displays to add dramatic flourish. The
design decisions for the three-tier restaurant, housed in
a brownstone on NoHo's happening Bond Street,
include the use of bare walnut floors and tables, a grid
of rafters hanging from the ceiling, geometric paper
sconces and unadorned walls.

COCKTAILS
BRANDY ALEXANDER
FRENCH 75
PIMMS CUP
GIN RANDY

CHAMPAGNE COCKTA
NEGRONI
BLOOD ORANGE COSM
SIDECAR
BLOOD ORANGE MARGA

DINER STYLE

94 **Diner**

4 85 Broadway

Diner, epicenter of ultra-hip Williamsburg, is an uncontested mecca of cool. Ever since co-owners Andrew Tarlow and Mark Firth refurbished this battered 1927 dining car in 1999, artists and fashionistas from an ever-increasing radius have colonized its leaning banquettes on Sunday mornings or late Friday nights, to view themselves and each other nonchalantly in the bar-length strip of mirror. The music is loud – there's a DJ on weekend evenings – the air hazed by Camel Light smoke and the mullet-haired staff have just the right mix of friendliness and reserve. With its wobbly bar stools, cracked mosaic flooring and bunches of fresh flowers on the bar, Diner manages to retain an indefinable essence of run-down charm. The plastic-clad menu lists its good-value foods generically – "green salad," "spinach" or "burger" – in a suitably basic Courier font. The waiting staff will scrawl in ballpoint pen on your table's paper covering Caroline Fidanza's Contemporary American specials, such as perfectly cooked whole trout or codfish hash.

94 **Peter Luger's Steakhouse**

5 178 Broadway

The favored way to arrive at this infamous Brooklyn steak house is by limousine. Fur coats and fat wallets congregate daily to gorge what is generally deemed to be the best porterhouse steak in the country. The 1887 eatery, originally called Charles Luger's Café, Billiard and Bowling Alley and patronized by local shipyard workers, was purchased in 1950 by Sol Forman, a regular customer who owned a metalworking plant across the street; his descendants still run the place. Veteran waiters gruffly play their parts in a no-nonsense, yet consciously theatrical dining experience: menus are reserved for first-timers only, knives and forks, plates and napkins are flung rather than placed on the bare oak tables. It is the Iowa corn-fed beef, however, that is the star performer of the show. Sizzling shortloins, dry-aged on the premises, are served for two, three or four on platters ritualistically tilted so that the waiter can spoon a mixture of butter and meat juices over your chunks of tender meat. The only way to leave Peter Luger's is sated.

34 | **Corner Bistro**

37 | 331 West 4th Street

It's 2:00 a.m., you're with friends and you've had a few drinks; your mind has fixed upon the idea of a burger. Your course is set for this dark and divey sports bar where cheeseburgers and chicken sandwiches served on paper plates with all the essential condiments cost $4 and $5.50 respectively. The jukebox is well stocked with mournful music, and McSorley's ale is only $2 a glass. Style and Corner Bistro are words that do not sit easily together – the clientele is regrettably of the Frat boy variety – but this atmospheric corner tavern, located at the point in Manhattan's West Village where the street grid system breaks down most fully, is a great place to watch a game or simply nurse a bourbon on the rocks at the bar to the tune of Tom Waits.

MENU

BISTRO BURGER   500

HAMBURGER   450

CHEESEBURGER   475

GRILLED CHICKEN   500
SANDWICH   275
GRILLED CHEESE   400
    WITH BACON   400
                     400

BLT   575
CHILI   200
CHILI BURGER
FRENHC FRIES

OYSTER VAULT

66 Oyster Bar at Grand Central Station

3 Grand Central Station, Lower Concourse, 42nd Street

Don't be put off by the early 1980s rainbow graphics on the door; this place is timeless. Lunchtimes are best. A canny waitress, who slides fresh biscuits and butter at you the minute you pick a white leatherette seat at one of the U-shaped counters, will serve your food fast and hard. But take your time and soak it all up: recently cleaned Guastavino vaulted ceilings, tiled floor and an enormous paper menu of oysters harvested from all over North America and being shucked in big tubs at a side bar. The clientele includes few travelers (most train riders choose the blander fast-food concessions on the food court above); instead it is the lunchtime refuge of midtown businessmen and quintessential New York characters who'll "take the usual, please, Jeannie," whether that's a clam chowder, an oyster pan roast or a dozen Blue Points.

BRIGHT LIGHTS, BIG CITY

14 Odeon

5 145 West Broadway

The 1930s substructure of this restaurant interior is still visible after a 1980 renovation at the hands of fraternal restaurant stylists Brian and Keith McNally and owner Lynn Wagenknecht. Original fixtures such as the granite floor, the Art Déco wood paneling and pendant globe lights remain. As Jay McInerney understates in *Bright Lights, Big City*, the Odeon "makes you feel reasonable at any hour, often against bad odds." The afternoon brings light, severed into strips by Venetian blinds, to a Bloody Mary brunch and the small hours see a lively crew of fashion and art types crowded into red and black leather banquettes for good American bistro fare.

THEATRICAL DINING

 Town

 15 West 56th Street

After a cocktail in the semicircular balcony lounge, diners descend a dramatic switchback staircase to the dining area below. The space that soars to 24 feet (over 7 meters) at its highest point bears many of the signature marks of New York's most prolific restaurant design hothouse, the Rockwell Group. Theatrical touches, such as strands of light-catching crystal beads suspended from the ceiling, the use of richly colored fabrics and backlit anigre wood panels behind the banquettes, are used to charm rather than bedazzle the senses. Owner and chef Geoffrey Zakarian's New American cooking style is elegant and clean. Dishes such as risotto of escargots with black truffle broth and duck steak with fragrant endive and soba buckwheat pilaf are typical of this fine example of hotel dining located in the Chambers.

You will find this small and quirky restaurant, which shares the chef and owner's childhood nickname, by following the long line that trails along East 1st Street. Especially popular with brunchers – it offers the particularly fine Chicago Matchbox Bloody Mary accompanied by a kebab of crunchy pickled vegetables and a chaser of Red Stripe in a shot glass – Prune is an intimate restaurant that evokes a Parisian bistro, despite its New American menu. Appetizers, such as a dish of fresh figs served with Serrano ham and pan-fried almonds, and main dishes, such as duck breast served with a small omelette flavored with rye, are irreverent and suitable for an interior that features wobbly wooden tables and naked-lady drinking glasses.

Gage and Tollner

13 372 Fulton Street

At dusk each evening a uniformed waiter proceeds
down a 100-foot-long (30-meter) central aisle of the
Pullman dining car-like interior of a Brooklyn oyster
and chop house and, with a long wick, he ignites the
gas lights that drop from elaborately wrought brass
chandeliers. Their diffused light reflects in the rows of
tall arched mirrors set in mahogany framework and
velvet brocade wall panels. This remarkable time
capsule, which predates the completion of the Brooklyn
Bridge by four years, is Gage and Tollner. Today, the
landmark Italianate façade, with its Doric column-
flanked portico, sits rather uncomfortably in a street of
neon-lit 99-cent stores. Push through the mahogany and
etched-glass revolving door, sit down to a feast of classic
American fare with a southern twist, such as she-crab
soup, steak or fried oysters atop a mushroom-fennel
ragout, however, and you will be quite literally
transported to Brooklyn's belle époque.

"I'LL HAVE WHAT SHE'S HAVING"

Katz's Deli

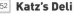 205 East Houston Street

A stalwart institution of the Jewish Lower East Side since 1888, Katz's delicatessen is the place to satisfy your cravings for hot pastrami and corned-beef sandwiches. Favored by presidents – even Bill Clinton's famously large appetite was apparently satiated after a sandwich (plus two more to take back to Washington, DC), it is also popular among actors – Meg Ryan famously demonstrated her fake orgasm in *When Harry Met Sally* at one of Katz's Formica tables. The air is thick with the smell of hanging salamis and pickles and the bustle of regulars who handle the obstacle course necessary to obtain a sandwich with wisecracking ease.

14 Chanterelle

6 2 Harrison Street

This grandly proportioned space – once the site of the Mercantile Exchange – was remodeled in 1989 by owners Bill Katz and Karen Waltuck into an elegant, airy dining room. Seemingly immune to the vagaries of fashion that propel other of its TriBeCa neighbors into obsequious contortions, Chanterelle has retained the same classic interior ever since. Its features include magnificent floral arrangements and widely spaced tables simply set with white linen and china. Large windows are half covered with sheer curtains and the reception area walls are hung with pieces of art by the likes of Cindy Sherman and Cy Twombly. The menu, which changes every four weeks, features hearty French dishes such as beef fillet with oysters and oyster sauce.

CAFÉ CULTURE

14 Café Gitane

20 242 Mott Street

Beautiful people gather at Café Gitane – lots of them, so expect a long line. And while the calculated insouciance of the young Italian photographer at the next table, showing contact sheets to an Austrian art director, can be a little grating, you'll forgive and forget as soon as you settle into this delightful café. With a delicate Moroccan glass of fresh mint tea in hand and a towering sandcastle of couscous to come, you can lean back amid the eddy of NoLIta activity and bask in the afternoon sun streaming in across the tiled floor.

52 Craft

5 43 East 19th Street

Diners can literally craft their own meals at this innovative New American restaurant. Tom Colicchio's refreshingly back-to-basics approach to cooking puts some of the onus on the diner. You have to choose whether you want your meat, fish or vegetables to be roasted, braised or sautéed and which of the side dishes – large and served family-style in copper pots and casseroles – you'd like to complement them. The interior of Craft glows. Warmth emanates from large, cherry-wood tables. The soft light of orange-filament Ferrowatt bulbs is reflected from the imbuia wood floor. Inspired by his collection of brass objects designed by the Austrian Carl Aubock, Craft's interior designer, Peter Bentels, chose bronze for the front door, bathroom sinks and interior metal accents – a welcome respite from the hard-edged aluminium and cool stainless steel of too many restaurant interiors of the past few years.

drink

New York runs on two liquid fuels. By day, the steam that leaks through its manholes seems to come from some giant subterranean espresso machine fixing the city's inhabitants with its nerve-jangling energy. Towards day's end, it is the cocktails that provide the high: Gimlets, Gibsons, Cosmopolitans, Manhattans, Highballs, French 75s – the very names ooze nostalgia. Measures don't exist and the art of mixology is highly evolved. Imbibing in New York is a specialized activity, with particular bars for particular beverages, moods and times of the day or night. And the nights can be long: most bars stay open until 4:00 a.m.

52

Good World Barber Shop

30 3 Orchard Street

When this Swedish-run bar in a former Chinese barbershop opened it seemed impossibly far away from the action. The interior is spare, with industrial-grade wooden floors and plain wooden tables and only a large moose head on the wall behind the bar for decoration. Climb on one of the tall barstools for a mean Aquavit martini and bar snacks, such as toast skagen made of white fish roe and Norwegian shrimp in a light lemon dill and sour-cream sauce, served on a toasted sourdough baguette or salmon rolls. DJs play most nights of the week and there is a small yard out back.

52 **Teany**

19 90 Rivington Street

With 90 blends of tea, some harder alternatives such as Champagne mojitos and sangria, a mod all-white, glass and chrome interior and tunes mixed by the musician himself, you don't have to abstain from much to enjoy Moby's vegetarian sanctuary. Melville Hall is a hands-off owner, leaving the menu choices and the day-to-day running of the café to his partner and fellow vegan, Kelly Tisdale.

BEER, SPIT AND SAWDUST
McSorley's Old Ale House

52

14 15 East 7th Street

"There is a thick musty smell that acts as a balm to jerky nerves; it is really a rich compound of the smells of pine sawdust, tap drippings, pipe tobacco, coal smoke, and onions." So wrote Joseph Mitchell in his 1942 book *McSorley's Wonderful Saloon*. These days the best time to visit the Ale House is the afternoon, when shafts of sunlight slice through the dense atmosphere and you can banter with the Irish barkeeps. First opened in 1854, it took 116 years for the establishment to allow women to pass the threshold.

CALIFORNIAN THEME PARK

34 | **The Park**

24 | 118 Tenth Avenue

Nightlife impresarios Sean McPherson (Bar Marmont in L.A.) and Eric Goode (Area and B-Bar in New York) hired design guru Jim Walrod to conceive their latest restaurant and lounge. They took three taxi garages and turned them into an enormous theme park where the interior references country lodge and opium den in equal measure. A Dracaena tree, gold-dipped Mies van der Rohe Barcelona chairs, giant benches cut from tree trunks and crackling fires – all add their own notes and contribute to a rare oasis in an industrial West Chelsea setting.

WINE AND CHEESE

Sherwood Café at Robin des Bois

7 195 Smith Street

After outfitting many of Manhattan's better-known French bistros, Bernard Decanali opened a café of his own in his Boerum Hill antiques shop. In the summer the leafy garden, with its eclectic assortment of seating and old enamel advertising signage, is a great place for a few bottles of wine and fantastic snacking fare. Inside, the crazy collection of objects – such as stuffed crocodiles, 1950s hatstands and chandeliers, stacked Parisian salon–style from floor to ceiling – combines with a clientele that easily mixes families and local hipsters.

Caffé Roma

 385 Broome Street

Look in the compendium of New York Saturday afternoon pastimes, and under "H" for heavenly you'll find a thimble-full of strong espresso and a Sicilian-style cannoli from one of Little Italy's oldest pasticcerias. Sit at a marble-topped table near the window and watch the bustle go by. Relics of late-19th-century Little Italy, such as the pressed-tin ceiling, a saloon clock that hangs over the espresso machine and the wooden back bar behind the take-away pastry counter, remain undisturbed thanks to the long-time family running of the business.

34 **Passerby**

21 436 West 15th Street

Fortunately, this bar's regulars have managed to defend it against the attacks of marauding "bridge-and-tunnelers," so it is still possible to lean on the long bar with artists from gallery owner Gavin Brown's celebrated stable, such as Elizabeth Peyton, Chris Ofili and Udomsak Krisanamis. The room's raw interior, designed by artist Mark Handforth, features a bar made from wood that furniture designer George Nakashima had, before he died, intended for a dining table. A multicolored disco floor by Piotr Uklanski pulses to the beat of some of the city's best DJs.

MIDTOWN MERRIMENT

66 King Cole Bar and Lounge
14 St. Regis Hotel, 2 East 55th Street

Legend has it that this dark and magical bar tucked off the lobby of the swanky St. Regis hotel is the birthplace of the Bloody Mary, which here goes by its original name, the Red Snapper. After a couple of these potent, spicy concoctions, accompanied by liberal servings of salted almonds and macadamia nuts, you will feel that you are, like the eponymous nursery-rhyme hero of the bar's spectacular mural by Frederick Maxfield Parrish, a "merry old soul." The wood-paneled warmth and the deep banquettes provide refuge from the crowds of Fifth Avenue.

LATE NIGHT SAKE
14 Chibi's Sake Bar
30 238 Mott Street

Chibi's proprietor, Marja Samsom, named the bar after her French bulldog, who likes to lounge in a corner of the main room and can be seen on special occasions skateboarding on the sidewalk outside. Bar staff will help you distinguish an Umenishiki from a Nanbu Toji when you order your sake and will advise on the relative merits of a Chibitini versus a Saketini. Snacks include Japanese delicacies, Kumamoto oysters and mushroom dumplings. This is a laid-back Zen drinking den, good for small groups late at night.

66 **Cellar Bar**

7 The Bryant Park, 40 West 40th Street

Located beneath the former American Radiator Building, an exemplar of Gothic Revival style designed by Raymond Hood in 1924 and immortalized by artist Georgia O'Keeffe until it was refashioned as a hotel by London architect David Chipperfield, this cavernous vault bar takes its theme and attitude from Bryant Park—a location it shares with New York Fashion Week. The models' drink of choice is the Razmopolitan, made with Absolut Citron, Cointreau, raspberry syrup and homemade lemon sour – the neon hues of which are reflected in the lighting design.

CLANDESTINE COCKTAILS

52 **Angel's Share**

13 8 Stuyvesant Street

It is a combination of strict house rules – no standing, no groups of more than four, no shouting – and an out-of-the-way location at the rear of a second-floor fluorescent-lit Japanese restaurant that helps screen the crowds at this jewel of a bar. For even more privacy, seek out the curtained-off section at the end of the narrow space. The old-school cocktails are mixed with cool precision by some of the most skilled bartenders in town. Named for the portion of alcohol that's lost to the "angels" during the ageing process, this bar breathes nothing but refinement.

High ceilings, a long bar and velvet curtains provide the perfect 1940s movie-palace setting for a well-mixed martini before a showing of *Breakfast at Tiffany's*. Both the bar and the movie theater were designed by Larry Bogdanow, whose other creations include the Cub Room and the Union Square Café. Taking the concept of dinner and a movie at its most literal and elegant extreme, try the reasonably priced three-course prix-fixe menu and a movie ticket, which includes a bag of treats for the show.

14 Mare Chiaro

13 176 Mulberry Street

Among the few remnants of an ever-dwindling Little Italy neighborhood is a small, cigar-smoke-filled bar-cum-social club dubbed, somewhat inappropriately, Mare Chiaro. Most of the cigar smoke comes from owner Tony Tenneriello's ever-smoldering Cuban, as he sits on his stool surveying the customers from under hooded eyes. While the cheap beer, sawdust-strewn floor and Formica dinner tables smack of a dive bar, its legendary clientele, including the late Frank Sinatra, and its starring role in movies, such as *The Godfather Part III* and *Donnie Brasco*, lend Mare Chiaro an aura of dusty mobster glamor.

EIGHTIES GLAM SCENE

14 B-Bar

59 40 East 4th Street

There is a scene in John Waters's 1998 film *Pecker* in which a young provincial photographer, discovered by an avaricious gallery owner, is heralded at a dinner by the New York art scene. The dinner takes place at the Bowery Bar – the perfect location for Waters's satirical portrait of the city's art-world elite. The bar and its rainbow light-bedecked patio was once a gas station on the city's most famously down-and-out street. Converted in the 1980s by Eric Goode and Serge Becker, it now hosts club-nights, such as "Beige," Erich Conrad's celebrity-studded gay extravaganza.

POWER-DRINKING

66 Four Seasons Bar

10 The Seagram Building, 99 East 52nd Street

A drink at the Four Seasons Bar, designed in 1959 by Philip Johnson and located in Mies van der Rohe's Seagram building, should be taken in direct proportion to the high seriousness and urbanity of its setting. If you're not already suited and tied along with the rest of the power-crowd, the maitre d' will provide you with a nylon jacket and tie. Check out the gold-anodized aluminum chain window coverings designed by Marie Nichol that undulate softly in the breeze of the ventilation system and Richard Lippold's sculpture of brass rods, which hangs portentously over the bar like so many swords of Macbeth.

CHURCH OF VODKA

14 Temple Bar

65 332 Lafayette Street

Like some strange clue in an Indiana Jones movie, the silhouette of an iguana skeleton on the wall at 332 Lafayette Street is the Temple Bar's only marker. Inside, the plush dark interior, magnificent cherry-oak bar, black marble and dim Déco sconces are seductively enveloping. Try one of a massive collection of vodkas with a bowl of spicy popcorn or choose from a bar menu that includes fresh oysters on the half shell, Beluga caviar, salmon canapés and Angus steak skewers. Then try to leave. You'll find that time has its own measure in this alcohol-hazed shrine.

shop

From the gargantuan department stores of Madison Avenue to the waif-sized boutiques that cluster along Elizabeth, Rivington, Perry, Bond Streets and Bedford Avenue, or wherever the breeze of fashion blows them, New York provides the material — both raw and ready-to-wear — from which entire lifestyles can be assembled. As the selection below attests, a rich spectrum of retail experiences awaits: classics; shops where the interiors are as fashionable as the wares they house; and a new variety that blends the essences of shop, gallery and museum. Prepare to be pleasantly confused.

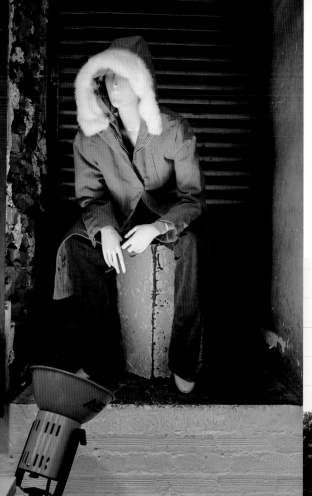

STYLE IMMERSION

80 **Barneys**

2 660 Madison Avenue

At this axis of New York style (with the most decadent of Christmastime window displays in town) you'll indulge in a truly luxurious shopping experience that spans nine floors displaying thousands of products and ends with lunch and top-quality people-watching at Fred's restaurant on the basement level. Minimalist architect Peter Marino was commissioned in 1993 by the Pressman family to convert the 1955 building at Madison Avenue and 61st Street into the 230,000 square feet (21,350 square meters) of unmissable New York event that Barneys is today.

UPTOWN BARGAINS

34 **Barneys Co-op**

9 236 West 18th Street and 116 Wooster Street

The downtown branches of the infamous uptown department store carry labels such as Daryl K, Katayone Adeli, Jill Stuart and Vivienne Tam, proportionately less expensive and more street-inspired than those stocked by their uptown big sister. If you are in the city in August or February you are in for the fashion spectacle known as the Barney's Warehouse Sale, when the 18th Street store makes way for clothes with prices slashed up to 80 per cent. Watch out for a stampede of well-heeled women trying to get to that sexy Marc Jacobs secretary cashmere cardigan.

94 | ISA

3 | 88 North 6th Street

This modern salon was a welcome arrival to the Williamsburg fashion scene, which, until Isa Saalabi opened shop, had had to make do solely with vintage and thrift. The concrete space often hosts street-spilling parties for labels such as ORFI, exhibitions of Brooklyn-grown artists such as RoStarr and DJ nights. ISA caters for men with tough denims, sweaters and T-shirts and for women with a good selection of big- and small-name designers (United Bamboo, Marc by Marc Jacobs), local artists (M.R.S.) and hard-to-find pieces (originals from DHBJR).

Sigerson Morrison
 28 Prince Street

Kari Sigerson's and Miranda Morrison's line of mint-green lined shoes have been a hit with the ladies who lunch ever since they opened their small store in NoLIta eight years ago. The larger new location, once a vegetable warehouse, features a storefront grid of aluminium, glass and white "penny tile," which affords enticing views of the luminous interior. Inside, movable brushed-steel tables display their signature kitten-heeled mules and buckled pumps and a long red banquette designed for Cappellini by Miranda's brother, Jasper.

FASHION SUPERMARKET
14 **Kirna Zabete**
51 96 Greene Street

Beth Buccini and Sarah Easley are the minds behind this fascinatingly eclectic SoHo store, which they tout as a "saccharine-free supermarket of style." In 1999 they commissioned Nick Dine to design the rainbow interior, which includes a lavender resin floor, pink uplights and cornflower-blue neoprene seats. Its racks loaded with pieces by avant-garde designers such as Bruce, Martine Sitbon and Matthew Williamson, this original boutique has garnered a devoted fashion following. There is even a range of designer pet paraphernalia downstairs.

STREET-STYLE GENERAL STORE

 Steven Alan

1 103 Franklin Street

This TriBeCa emporium of emerging designers was conceived as an old-fashioned general store, with rolling ladders that slide along ceiling-high wooden shelves stacked with La cosa T-shirts and a 1940s pharmacy display case containing Dr Hauschka cosmetic products. Labels are from the likes of APC, Wink, Martin Margiela 6 and Katayone Adeli. An upholstered bench is flanked by two listening stations whose sample sounds are changed biweekly by the people at Other Music (p. 31).

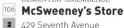
A *Wunderkammer* of oddities at the dustier end of Brooklyn's Park Slope, this place displays the true spirit of Dave Eggers's *McSweeney's* publishing enterprise and online "Internet Tendency," and defies categorization, despite the elaborate Dewey decimal labeling system applied to its deliciously bizarre inventory. There are racks that include such sought-after journals as *American Window Cleaner Magazine* and *Coal Age*. Open drawers to find intricate *in media res* dioramas of chess-playing Tyrannosaurus Rex models. Reach up to vertiginously stacked shelves and cabinets to retrieve a cast-pewter pelican foot ($5.00), a Feline dental exam label ($0.20), an eyedropper ($0.99) or a Bitch Creek nymph fly, size eight ($4.74). Rent tapdancing shoes by the hour. The store also stocks back issues of the *McSweeney's* journal, associated publications such as *Might* magazine and other titles by Eggers and his crew of *McSweeney's* authors. And, should the cabinet prove just too curious for comfort, store manager Scott Seeley or one of the interns perched behind a high counter will politely answer your questions.

When partners Renata Bokalo and Roman Luba opened their pitch-perfect designer lifestyle store in 1999, they also pioneered a retail revolution in the Meatpacking District. The area is now New York's design and fashion Grand Central – much to the bemusement of the few remaining meat packers still operating in the area. Auto features the work of Brooklyn-based designers who manage to combine craftsmanship and knowing modernity in their household objects and accessories: leather flowers by Red Head Amy, stitched pillows by Judy Ross, and much much more.

Former fashion entrepreneur Murray Moss's white-cube, industrial-product-design store in SoHo blurs the distinction between museum and shop. The covetable porcelain tableware, crystal and cutlery are forcefully presented in thematic association with one another – rather than in terms of function and material – and contextualized with furniture and lighting. One may find, for instance, a Hella Jongerius ceramic pot next to a stainless-steel Fisher space pen next to an Edra pink leather Flap sofa. Most are contained in glass vitrines or on raised daises.

Bond 07

7 Bond Street

Tunisian-born Selima Salaun has a veritable empire of New York stores featuring her signature quirky sensibility and range of acid-bright eyeglasses. The latest is a gem of a boutique on 25 Prince Street called Lunettes et Chocolat, which takes niche retailing to a delightful extreme by selling only eyeglasses and delicious handmade chocolates. Another of her creations is Le Corset Boutique on 80 Thompson Street, which specializes in gorgeously over-the-top lingerie and loungewear. Bond 07, yet another of her coterie, is situated on NoHo's hip Bond Street (Daryl K and Ghost are among the storefronts that punctuate the brick-and-marble-trimmed row houses and quirky residential lofts). This one-stop shop for stylists focuses on a handpicked selection of accessories, such as hats and vintage Cartier, Rolex and Gucci watches.

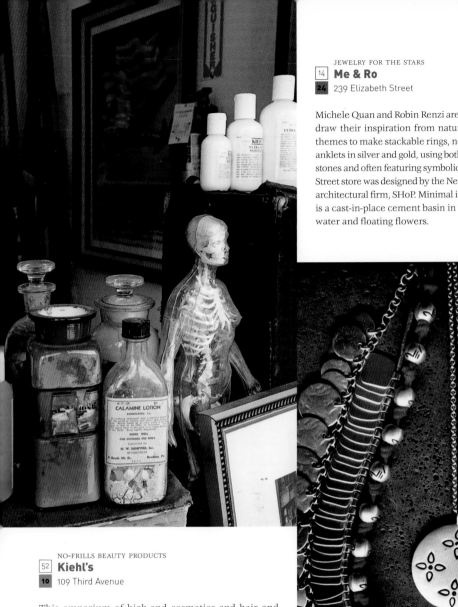

Me & Ro

`14` `24` 239 Elizabeth Street

Michele Quan and Robin Renzi are jewelry designers who draw their inspiration from nature and Middle Eastern themes to make stackable rings, necklaces, bracelets and anklets in silver and gold, using both semiprecious and rare stones and often featuring symbolic carving. This Elizabeth Street store was designed by the New York–based vanguard architectural firm, SHoP. Minimal in design, its one fanfare is a cast-in-place cement basin in the window filled with water and floating flowers.

NO-FRILLS BEAUTY PRODUCTS

Kiehl's

`52` `10` 109 Third Avenue

This emporium of high-end cosmetics and hair and skincare products – the formulae for which have been passed down through the generations since the store opened as an apothecary's in 1851 – is an integral part of New York's heritage. White-lab-coated staff ply you with samples and, using the same plain speaking as the products' no-frills packaging, answer your every beauty-related query. The setting is bizarre: half of the shop houses a collection of vintage motorcycles set on a floral rug before a wall of photographs of customers' babies.

Rem Koolhaas's retail laboratory for Prada arrived in a flurry of media attention in late 2001. Its position at the hub of SoHo and the fact that it runs a whole block means that you can hardly miss it. Its imagination-catching features include the "wave," a concave shape lined with polished zebra wood that runs the length and height of the store; a glass elevator that displays merchandise; and a baroquely wallpapered north wall created by graphic designers 2 x 4. Groundbreaking technological gadgets abound in this "museum show on indefinite display."

Spade's signature all-terrain canvas and waxwear bags and jackets and notebooks are presented back-to-back with vintage props such as Braun turntables, *Playboy* magazines, globes and balsa-wood aeroplanes in this 500-square-foot (46-square-meter) SoHo space designed by Stephen Sclaroff. The well-curated collection is the work of Andy Spade (Kate's husband; see p. 175) and might well stand as New York's riposte to Paul Smith.

This loft-style NoLIta store contains a few rolling racks of clean, beautifully cut men's and women's Egyptian cotton button-down shirts and a magnificent Tascam 32 reel-to-reel tape machine. The back third of the store is devoted to the shop's first-rate made-to-measure business. The look of the suits, jackets, trousers and shirts is modern and clean, but husband-and-wife team James and Gwendolyn Jurney use old-world tailoring techniques, such as single-needle stitching for the shirts, and the suits are mostly handsewn.

34 **Marc Jacobs**

34 • Marc by Marc Jacobs, 403 Bleecker Street
• Marc Jacobs Men's Store, 405 Bleecker Street

Despite his international success and residence in Paris, Marc Jacobs – who trained at New York's Parsons School of Design – truly belongs to this city. Barneys's painted advertising hoardings once declared, "We Love Marc Jacobs" and Manhattan's best-dressed people show no signs of letting their devotion dwindle. These outpost stores were designed by Stephen Jaklitsch and are nestled on the most gorgeous two-block stretch of Bleecker Street (between Bank and Perry Streets) among Magnolia Bakery,

Lulu Guinness and the flower shop with the beautiful window displays. One carries the company's popular secondary line, Marc, which features accessories such as his signature chunky latched and zippered handbags and Minnie Mouse-style pumps and flats. The other houses the Marc Jacobs men's range.

In an exquisitely assembled boutique in the heart of NoLIta, Brit designer and ex-model Jane Mayle and her gorgeous assistants sell lace dresses and fluttery silk floral blouses that you can pair with librarian-chic leather-edged tweed skirts. Among the racks of this sweet-smelling store – Mayle was responsible for initiating the craze for Votivo redcurrant candles – are showcased accessories and other objets d'art such as a Julian Schnabel exhibition poster from 1989. Mayle says her work is inspired by the style of 1950s Italian film star Monica Vitti, whose wardrobe defined feminine elegance. Courtney Love and Sofia Coppola are among the fans of Mayle's off-the-shoulder chemises and crocheted shawls.

MYTHICAL MERCHANDISE

 Castor and Pollux

 67 ½ Sixth Avenue

Co-owners Anne-Catherine Lüke and Kerrilynn Hunt are the ladies with the shared vision behind this intimate boutique. Their combined interior design and fashion expertise infuses both the visual character of the store – which they composed themselves from customized fixtures and antiques – and the carefully honed trove of whimsical accessories and clothing that it stows. Clutch wallets by Abas, jewelry by Melissa Joy Manning and a range of classic underwear by On Gossamer are juxtaposed with the kinds of objects that, as they put it, "you would find

in one of our apartments." Lüke and Hunt design their own signature line that puts ladylike chic in an urban context. Although the store is situated in a somewhat in-between neighborhood of Brooklyn, it's definitely worth the expedition, especially if you can attend one of the friendly soirées that introduce each new season's collection.

14 **Kate Spade Travel**

33 59 Thompson Street

Now that handbag entrepreneur Kate Spade has become a global brand — which includes clothing, shoes, luggage, eyeglasses, and paper collections – the roots of her phenomenally successful business appear all the more tinged with nostalgia. In the beginning, back in 1993, she sold only six simple shapes of bag that emphasized utility, color and fabric. Number 59 Thompson Street is the location of Spade's very first shop, whose pretty storefront now houses Kate Spade Travel, representing the refined essence of her much-expanded label. Here you'll find whimsical travel accessories for the modern woman, including hot-water-bottle covers, erasers, colorful notebooks and wallets, vintage scarves and quality luggage in black or striped canvas.

retreat

New Yorkers know that weekend-long releases from the pressure of the city are essential for their long-term survival. Luckily for the time-deficient — visitors and residents alike — a mere 100-mile (160-kilometer) radius of Manhattan encompasses a topographical variety with ample potential for both active and contemplative diversion: from the sea-level shenanigans of the Hamptons to the high-altitude hippy hangouts of the Catskill Mountains, from the history-rich rolling pastures of Bucks County in Pennsylvania to the art-world destination found in the deep wooded valley carved by the Hudson River.

Catskills: A Countercultural Escape

- Storm King Art Center
- Café Tamayo
- The Villa at Saugerties

The Catskill Mountains is a spectacular wilderness, which, with Woodstock as its unofficial capital, is the counterculture's retreat of choice. The area has also caught the attention of those New Yorkers recently priced out of the Hamptons and now casting about for an alternative Arcadia. To join them, from Manhattan, take the George Washington Bridge to the Palisades Parkway North for a scenic drive up the west bank of the Hudson River. Make a stop at Storm King Art Center, a magnificent sculpture park that ranges over 500 acres (200 hectares) of landscaped lawns, fields and woodlands ornamented by monumental pieces by postwar American and European artists such as Alexander Calder, David Smith and Andy Goldsworthy, whose stone wall, winding in and out of the trees, is worth the trip alone.

Further into the Catskills is the small town of Saugerties, the site of the second 1960s Woodstock rock festival and home to those quintessential American main streets. Yes, there are antiques shops but they are interspersed with a bay-windowed candy shop, a hardware store with its brightly colored wheelbarrows upended on the sidewalk and an old-fashioned cinema. The small selection of restaurants includes a great place called Café Tamayo, offering New American bistro fare in an interior decorated with 1800s paddle fans.

The Villa at Saugerties is a contemporary bed and breakfast in a 1929 Spanish-style villa with an ochre stucco exterior and red tile roof, set in a pastoral setting down a back road outside the town. Owners Aimee Szparaga and Richard Nocera are young Manhattanites who recently upped sticks to set up a "modern country escape." With its palette of grey and magenta, the living area has modern Danish pieces and features an exposed bluestone fireplace Details such as bunches of fresh flowers, Jonathan Adler throw cushions and copies of *Visionaire* magazine ease discerning urbanites into their country refuge. In clement weather guests can eat breakfast underneath a spreading sycamore tree on the patio outside, near the pristine swimming pool.

The bucolic meadows, covered bridges and stone farmhouses of Bucks County in eastern Pennsylvania have long held artists and writers in thrall. In the 1930s and 1940s, New York's literati made the towns dotted along the Delaware River the scene of their voluntary exile. Dorothy Parker, the acerbic wit of the Algonquin Round Table, gravitated to a 14-room manse in Piperville, and Oscar Hammerstein, the lyricist, resettled on a farm in Doylestown. Today, while the town of New Hope has become rather touristy, there is still plenty for those with a curiosity for whimsical history, antiques and art or just beautiful countryside.

Install yourself at the EverMay on the Delaware, a three-story, 18-room inn dating from 1790 and set right beside the river. Each room, amply furnished with antiques, is named for a famous person in Bucks County history. The stately Colonel William Erwin room, for example, sports a baronial headboard and matching marble-topped bureau. The six-course, award-winning dinner is the work of chef Jeffrey Lauble.

Archaeologist, architect, fiddler, tilemaker and erudite collector: Henry Chapman Mercer left his mark firmly upon Doylestown, where he spent all of his life. Mercer's dream house – a demented sandcastle of a mansion named Fonthill – which he built by hand between 1908 and 1912, is made from hand-poured reinforced concrete. As a leading figure of the Arts and Crafts movement, he established a tilemaking factory and Fonthill is lined with his handmade colorful, often narrative-depicting tiles. The Mercer Museum holds his collection of more than 50,000 tools of early American crafts and trades and everyday household objects used in America from 1700 to 1850. To add to your own collection of Americana, cross the river to Lambertville, an unpretentious town with a colonial-village feel and the site of the famous Lambertville Antique Market and Golden Nugget Antique Flea Market, both on River Road.

Hudson River Valley: Ancient Landscape, Contemporary Art

- Dia: Beacon
- Pig Hill Inn
- East Side Kitchen

Beacon is a small 18th- and 19th-century town on the banks of the River Hudson, 60 miles (100 kilometers) and so many fashion cycles north of Manhattan. And yet this sleepy town is the new home of Dia's permanent collection of major works of art from the 1960s to the present and thus a new hot spot on the international map of contemporary art. The museum – collaboratively planned by Robert Irwin, an art legend, and project architect, the New York-based Open Office – occupies a historic printing factory on the banks of the Hudson River. The 1929 steel, concrete and glass factory building provides a superb environment for contemporary art. The gritty industrial town itself is of interest too. A burgeoning art scene has brought artists and galleries to the warehouse buildings, and dozens of excellent antique shops flank the main street.

Beacon's riches do not, as yet, include any accommodations, so it is advisable to use as a base the quaint village of Cold Spring, some 10 miles (16 kilometers) to the south. Here too is a pleasing collection of antiques stores, book- and teashops lining the main street under ornate cornices. But the real treat lies at the end of the street, where it meets the Hudson River. The views – of the stretch up- and downstream where the river narrows and deepens and of the opposite bank, formed of primeval-looking masses of granite and dense green forest – are spectacular. Artists of the Hudson River School, such as Thomas Cole and Asher B. Durand, were similarly fascinated by this tract through the Appalachian Mountain range.

The Pig Hill Inn is the place to stay. Housed in an 1820 brick building on the main street, the inn has nine guest rooms, each appointed with antiques that are for sale, and most have wood stoves. Breakfast can be taken in your four-poster bed, the dining room or in the quiet garden out back. If you need a snack during the day, simply cross the street to the East Side Kitchen for a milkshake or burger in the playfully retro diner made over by a couple of East Village musicians.

Long Island's East End beaches are gorgeous broad swaths of pale sand, backed with low picket fences and dune grasses. Between the months of May and September, however, they are littered with high-strung New Yorkers "getting away from it all." Enormous ersatz mansions replete with back-garden polo fields for the likes of Sean "Puffy" Combs and Steven Spielberg have replaced the once-flat open potato fields that unfolded to the Atlantic. And yet, the clear light, the charm of clapboard villages such as Amagansett and the exhilarating sense of escape at Montauk, the South Fork's tip, ensure that the Hamptons remain a lovely retreat, particularly during September. East Hampton, with its boutiques and specialty shops, is easily accessible by bus or train and provides a good base. Just to the north, in a rural hamlet called The Springs, is the cottage and studio where Jackson Pollock created his most important works between 1946 and his death. The house has been left beautifully intact so that you can still browse the artist's large collection of jazz records and library and see the paint splatters on the floor. Bridgehampton, the next town to the west of East Hampton, is home to The Dan Flavin Art Institute, a permanent installation of nine of the artist's works in fluorescent light in a renovated firehouse building.

Most New Yorkers rent houses in the summer, and for short stays there are only a handful of interesting lodgings. One such place is Andre Balazs's 20-luxury-room Sunset Beach Hotel on Shelter Island, situated between the North and South Forks of Long Island. Another option is The 1770 House on East Hampton's Main Street, within easy reach of the boutiques and the secluded Egypt beach. Designer Laura Maerov, who recently restored the inn, has combined traditional wallpapers, wood paneling and eclectic antiques to give each room individual charm. The destination restaurant serves seasonal American cuisine by local star chef Kevin Penner.

contact

All telephone numbers are given for dialling locally, but a '1' must be dialled before the ten-digit number. From abroad, the country code is +1, followed by the ten-digit number (i.e., without another '1') Telephone numbers in the retreat section are given for dialling from New York: if calling from abroad, dial the country code (+1) plus the ten-digit number given. The number in brackets by the name is the page number on which the entry appears.

Abyssinian Baptist Church [90]
132 Odell Clark Place
New York, NY 10030
T   212 862 7474
F   212 862 3255
W   www.abyssinian.org

Ace Gallery [17]
275 Hudson Street
New York, NY 10013
T   212 255 5599

aka Cafe [60]
49 Clinton Street
New York, NY 10002
T   212 979 6096

Albanese Meats and Poultry [21]
238 Elizabeth Street
New York, NY 10012
T   212 966 1788

Algonquin Hotel [74]
59 West 44th Street
New York, NY 10036
T   212 840 6800
W   www.thealgonquin.net

Alife [58]
178 Orchard Street
New York, NY 10002
T   646 654 0628

Alife Rivington Club [58]
158 Rivington Street
New York, NY 10002
T   212 375 8128

Alpana Bawa [56]
41 Grand Street and
70 East 1st Street
New York, NY 10013
T   212 965 0559
F   212 965 0560
W   www.alpanabawa.com

American Folk Art Museum [75]
45 West 53rd Street
New York, NY 10019
T   212 265 1040
E   info@folkartmuseum.org
W   www.folkartmuseum.org

Anchorage [63]
Base of Brooklyn Bridge
Cadman Plaza West, at Hicks
and Old Fulton Streets
Brooklyn, NY 11201
T   212 206 6674
W   www.creativetime.org

Angel Orensanz Foundation Center for the Arts [60]
172 Norfolk Street
New York, NY 10002
T   212 780 0175
E   info@orensanz.org
W   www.orensanz.org

Angel's Share [156]
8 Stuyvesant Street
New York, NY 10003
T   212 777 5415

Annex Antiques Fair and Flea Market [38]
Sixth Avenue between 24th
and 26th Streets
New York, NY 10003
T   212 243 5343

The Apartment [27]
101 Crosby Street
New York, NY 10012
T   212 219 3661
F   212 219 3683
E   speakout@theapt.com
W   www.theapt.com

Apple Store [28]
103 Prince Street
New York, NY 10012
T   212 226 3126
W   www.apple.com/retail/soho

APT [44]
419 West 13th Street
New York, NY 10014
T   212 414 4245
E   info@aptwebsite.com
W   www.aptwebsite.com

Artists Space [22]
38 Greene Street, 3rd Floor
New York, NY 10013
T   212 226 3970
F   212 966 1434
E   artspace@artistsspace.org
W   www.artistsspace.org

Asia Society [83]
725 Park Avenue
New York, NY 10021
T   212 288 6400
F   212 517 8315
W   www.asiasociety.org

Auto [167]
805 Washington Street
New York, NY 10014
T   212 229 2292
F   212 517 8315
E   info@thisisauto.com
W   www.thisisauto.com

Balthazar [22]
80 Spring Street
New York, NY 10012
T   212 965 1785
F   212 966 2502
E   frontdesk@balthazarny.com
W   www.balthazarny.com

Bar 89 [22]
89 Mercer Street
New York, NY 10012
T   212 274 0989

Barney Greengrass Sturgeon King [136]
541 Amsterdam Avenue

New York, NY 10024
T   212 724 4707

Barneys [162]
660 Madison Avenue
New York, NY 10021
T   212 826 8900
W   www.barneys.com

Barneys Co-op [162]
236 West 18th Street
New York, NY 10011
116 Wooster Street
New York, NY 10012
T   212 593 7800
W   www.barneys.com

Bayard Building [31]
65 Bleecker Street
New York, NY 10012

B–Bar
(a.k.a. Bowery Bar)[158]
40 East 4th Street
New York, NY 10003
T   212 475 2220
F   212 475 9629
W   www.bbarandgrill.com

**Bed and Breakfast on
the Park** [116]
113 Prospect Park West
Brooklyn, NY 11215
T   718 499 6115
W   www.bbnyc.com

Bemelmans Bar [84]
Ground Floor of Carlyle Hotel
35 East 76th Street
New York, NY 10021
T   212 744 1600
W   www.thecarlyle.com

Bid [83]
1334 York Avenue
New York, NY 10021
T   212 988 7730

Bond 07 [168]
7 Bond Street
New York, NY 10012
T   212 677 8487
F   212 677 7872
W   www.selimaoptique.com

Bond Street [137]
6 Bond Street
New York, NY 10012
T   212 777 2500
F   212 777 6530

Bottino [40]
246 Tenth Avenue
New York, NY 10001
T   212 206 6766
E   info@bottinonyc.com
W   www.bottinonyc.com

Bouley [16]
120 West Broadway
New York, NY 10013
T   212 964 2525

E   bouleyrest@bouley.net
W   www.bouley.net

Brasserie [137]
100 East 53rd Street
New York, NY 10022
T   212 751 4840
W   www.restaurantassociates.
    com/brasserie

Bridge Cafe [63]
279 Water Street
New York, NY 10038
T   212 227 3344
F   212 619 2368

The Broken Kilometer [28]
393 West Broadway
New York, NY 10012
W   www.diacenter.org

**Brooklyn Academy
of Music** [111]
30 Lafayette Avenue
Brooklyn, NY 11217
T   718 636 4100
E   info@bam.org
W   www.bam.org

**Brooklyn Botanic
Garden** [108]
1000 Washington Avenue
Brooklyn, NY 11225
T   718 623 7200
W   www.bbg.org

Brooklyn Inn [108]
148 Hoyt Street
Brooklyn, NY 11217
T   718 625 9741

**Brooklyn Museum
of Art** [108]
200 Eastern Parkway
Brooklyn, NY 11238
T   718 638 5000
F   718 501 6134
E   information@
    brooklynmuseum.org
W   www.brooklynart.org

Café des Artistes [88]
1 West 67th Street
New York, NY 10023
T   212 877 3500
F   212 877 6263
W   www.cafedesartistesnyc.com

Café Gitane [146]
242 Mott Street
New York, NY 10012
T   212 334 9552

Café Habana [21]
17 Prince Street
New York, NY 10012
T   212 625 2001
F   212 625 3663

Café Lebowitz [21]
14 Spring Street
New York, NY 10012
T   212 219 2399

Café Luxembourg [89]
200 West 70th Street
New York, NY 10023
T   212 873 7411

Café Sabarsky [87]
Neue Galerie
1048 Fifth Avenue
New York, NY, 10028
T   212 288 0665
F   212 645 7127
W   www.wallserestaurant.com

Caffé Roma [154]
385 Broome Street
New York, NY 10013
T   212 226 8413

Calvin Klein [73]
654 Madison Avenue
New York, NY 10021
T   212 292 9000

Campbell Apartment [68]
Grand Central Terminal
Off the West Balcony
15 Vanderbilt Avenue
New York, NY 10017
T   212 953 0409

Castor and Pollux [174]
67 1/2 Sixth Avenue
New York, NY 10013
T/F 718 398 4141

Cellar Bar [156]
The Bryant Park
40 West 40th Street
New York, NY 10018
T   212 642 2260
W   www.bryantparkhotel.com

Centro Fly [37]
45 West 21st Street
New York, NY 10010
T   212 627 7770
E   mail@centro-fly.com
W   www.centro-fly.com

Chambers Hotel [130]
15 West 56th Street
New York, NY 10019
T   212 974 5656
F   212 974 5657
E   chambershotel@aol.com
W   www.chambershotel.com

Chanterelle [146]
2 Harrison Street
New York, NY 10013
T   212 966 6960
F   212 966 6143
E   information@
    chanterellenyc.com
W   www.chanterellenyc.com

Chelsea Market [38]
75 Ninth Avenue
New York, NY 10001
W   www.chelseamarket.com

Chibi's Sake Bar [155]
238 Mott Street

New York, NY 10012
T   212 274 0054
W   www.chibisbar.com

Chrysler Building [70]
405 Lexington Avenue
New York, NY 10174
T   212 682 3070

Church Lounge [18]
Tribeca Grand Hotel
2 Sixth Avenue
New York, NY 10013
T   212 519 6677
W   www.tribecagrand.com

City Bakery [55]
3 West 18th Street
New York, NY 10011
T   212 366 1414

City Club Hotel [124]
55 West 44th Street
New York, 10036
T   212 921 5500
F   212 944 5544
W   www.cityclubhotel.com

**C.O. Bigelow
Apothecaries** [48]
414 Sixth Avenue
New York, NY 10011
T   212 533 2700
W   www.bigelowchemists.com

Comme des Garçons [43]
520 West 22nd Street
New York, NY 10011
T   212 604 9200

Commissary [83]
1030 Third Avenue
New York, NY 10021
T   212 339 9955
F   212 339 0015
E   reservations
    @commissarynyc.com
W   www.commissarynyc.com

Conservatory Gardens [87]
Central Park
Fifth Avenue at 105th Street
New York
W   www.centralpark.org

**Cooper-Hewitt, National
Design Museum** [84]
2 East 91st Street
New York, NY 10128
T   212 849 8400
E   edu@si.edu
W   www.ndm.si.edu

Corner Bistro [140]
331 West 4th Street
New York, NY 10014
T   212 242 9502

Craft [147]
43 East 19th Street
New York, NY 10003
T   212 780 0880

Decibel Sake Bar [56]
240 East 9th Street
New York 10003
T   212 979 2733
W   www.sakebar.com

Deitch Projects [25]
76 Grand Street
New York, NY 10013
T   212 343 7300
18 Wooster Street
New York, NY 10013
T   212 941 9475

DIA Center for the Arts [41]
545 & 548 West 22nd Street
New York, NY 10011
T   212 989 5566
F   212 989 4055
W   www.diacenter.org

Diane von Furstenberg [48]
385 West 12th Street
New York, NY 10014
T   646 486 4800
W   www.dvf.com

Diner [138]
85 Broadway
Brooklyn, NY 11211
T   718 486 3077

Donald Judd House [24]
101 Spring Street
New York, NY 10012

Double Happiness [18]
173 Mott Street
New York, NY 10013
T   212 941 1282

Economy Candy [58]
108 Rivington Street
New York, NY 10002
T   212 254 1832
F   212 254 2606
W   www.economycandy.com

El Quijote [43]
226 West 23rd Street
New York, NY 10011
T   212 929 1855

Eyebeam Atelier [43]
540 West 21st Street
New York, NY 10012
T   718 222 3982
F   718 222 5621
W   www.eyebeam.org

Fanelli's [27]
94 Prince Street
New York, NY 10012
T   212 226 9412

First [57]
87 First Avenue
New York, NY 10003
T   212 674 3823

Flatiron Building [56]
175 Fifth Avenue
New York, NY 10010

Flight 001 [48]
96 Greenwich Avenue
New York, NY 10011
T   212 691 1001
F   212 691 8660
E   info@flight001.com
W   www.flight001.com

Florent [47]
69 Gansevoort Street
New York, NY 10014
T   212 989 5779
F   212 645 2498
W   www.restaurantflorent.com

Four Seasons Bar [159]
Seagram Building
99 East 52nd Street
New York, NY 10022
T   212 754 9494
F   212 754 1077
W   www.fourseasons
    restaurant.com

Frank's Lounge [111]
660 Fulton Street
Brooklyn, NY 11238
T   718 625 9339
W   www.frankscocktail
    lounge.com

Fraunces Tavern [63]
54 Pearl Street
New York, NY 10004
T   212 968 1776
F   212 797 1776
W   www.frauncestavern.com

Frick Collection [83]
1 East 70th Street
New York, NY 10021
T   212 288 0700
F   212 628 4417
E   info@frick.org
W   www.frick.org

Gage and Tollner [144]
372 Fulton Street
Brooklyn, NY 11201
T   718 875 5181
F   718 243 0222
E   gtollner@aol.com
W   www.gageandtollner.com

Gagosian [37]
555 West 24th Street
New York, NY 10011
T   212 741 1111
F   212 741 9611
E   info@gagosian.com
W   www.gagosian.com

Galapagos [99]
70 North 6th Street
Brooklyn, NY 11211
T   718 782 5188
E   info@galapagosartspace.com
W   www.galapagosartspace.com

**Gavin Brown's
Enterprise** [43]
436 West 15th Street

New York, NY 10011
T   212 627 5258

Good World Barber Shop
[150]
3 Orchard Street
New York, NY 10002
T   212 925 9975
W   www.goodworldbar.com

Gramercy Park Hotel [120]
2 Lexington Avenue
New York, NY 10010
T   212 475 4320
F   212 505 0535
W   www.gramercyparkhotel.com

Gramercy Tavern [55]
42 East 20th Street
New York, NY 10003
T   212 477 0777
F   212 477 1160

Grange Hall [48]
30 Commerce Street
New York, NY 10014
T   212 924 5246
F   212 255 2117

Greenmarket [97]
Union Square
East 17th Street and Broadway
New York, NY 10003
W   www.cenyc.org

Grocery [108]
288 Smith Street
Brooklyn, NY 11231
T   718 596 3335

Guastavino's [84]
409 East 59th Street
New York, NY 10022
T   212 980 2455
F   212 980 2904
W   www.guastavinos.com

Gucci [69]
685 Fifth Avenue
New York, NY 10022
T   212 826 2600
F   212 230 0894
W   www.gucci.com

Halcyon [108]
227 Smith Street
Brooklyn, NY 11231
T   718 260 9299
E   info@halcyonline.com
W   www.halcyonline.com

**Helmut Lang
Parfumerie** [28]
81 Greene Street
New York, NY 10012
T   212 334 3921
F   212 334 3922
W   www.helmutlang.com

**Henry Urbach
Architecture** [38]
526 West 26th Street, 10th Floor
New York, NY 10001

T   212 627 0974
F   212 645 7222
E   hua@huagallery.com
W   www.huagallery.com

Honmura An [28]
170 Mercer Street
New York, NY 10012
T   212 334 5253

Hotel Chelsea [126]
222 West 23rd Street
New York, NY 10011
T   212 243 3700
F   212 675 5531
W   www.hotelchelsea.com

INA [21]
Women's:
21 Prince Street
New York, NY 10012
T 212 334 9048
Men's:
262 Mott Street
New York, NY 10012
T 212 334 2210

The Inn at Irving Place [122]
56 Irving Place
New York, NY 10003
T   212 533 4600
F   212 533 4611
E   inn@innatirving.com
W   www.innatirving.com

**Isamu Noguchi Garden
Museum** [102]
32–37 Vernon Boulevard
Long Island City, NY 11106
T   718 204 7088
F   718 278 2348
[Temporary Space]
36–01 43rd Avenue
Long Island City, NY 11101
W   www.noguchi.org

ISA [163]
88 North 6th Street
Brooklyn, NY 11211
T   718 387 3363
F   718 387 3464

Jack Spade [170]
56 Greene Street
New York, NY 10012
T   212 625 1820
F   212 925 8477
W   www.jackspade.com

Jeffrey [47]
449 West 14th Street
New York, NY 10014
T   212 206 1272

Joe's Pub [31]
425 Lafayette Street
New York, NY 10003
T   212 539 8777
W   www.joespub.com

Juniors [111]
386 Flatbush Avenue

Brooklyn, NY 11238
T   718 852 5257

Kate Spade Travel [175]
59 Thompson Street
New York, NY 10012
T   212 965 8654
F   212 965 8653
W   www.katespade.com

Katz's Deli [145]
205 East Houston Street
New York, NY 10002
T   212 254 2246

Kiehl's [169]
109 Third Avenue
New York, NY 10003
T   212 677 3171
W   www.kiehls.com

**King Cole Bar and
Lounge** [155]
St. Regis Hotel
2 East 55th Street
New York NY 10022
T   212 753 4500
F   212 787 3447
W   www.starwood.com/stregis

Kirna Zabete [164]
96 Greene Street
New York, NY 10012
T   212 941 9656
E   info@kirnazabete.com
W   www.kirnazabete.com

Knitting Factory [18]
74 Leonard Street
New York, NY 10013
T   212 219 3006
W   www.knittingfactory.com

Kush [60]
183 Orchard Street
New York, NY 10002
T   212 677 7328

La Lunchonette [44]
130 Tenth Avenue
New York, NY 10011
T   212 675 0342

Language [21]
238 Mulberry Street
New York, NY 10012
T   212 431 5566
F   212 966 3994
E   service@language-nyc.com
W   www.language-nyc.com

Lenox Lounge [90]
288 Lenox Avenue (Malcolm
X Boulevard)
New York, NY 10027
T   212 427 0253
E   info@lenoxlounge.com
W   www.lenoxlounge.com

Li-Lac Chocolates, Inc. [48]
120 Christopher Street
New York, NY 10014

T   212 242 7374
F   212 366 5874

**Lincoln Center for the
Performing Arts** [89]
65th Street at Columbus Avenue
New York, NY 10023
T   212 875 5456
W   www.lincolncenter.org

Linda Dresner [72]
484 Park Avenue
New York, NY 10022
T   212 308 3177

Liz Christy Garden [31]
Northeast corner of Houston
and Bowery Streets
New York
W   www.lizchristygarden.org

Lot 61 [43]
550 West 21st Street
New York, NY 10011
T   212 243 6555
W   www.lot61.com

The Lowell [128]
28 East 63rd Street
New York, NY 10021
T   212 838 1400
F   212 605 6808

**Lower East Side Tenement
Museum** [60]
90 Orchard Street
New York, NY 10002
T   212 431 0233
F   212 431 0402
E   lestm@tenement.org
W   www.tenement.org

Luhring Augustine [38]
531 West 24th Street
New York, NY 10011
T   212 206 9100
F   212 206 9055
E   info@luhringaugustine.com
W   www.luhringaugustine.com

Luxx [101]
256 Grand Street
Brooklyn, NY 11211
T   718 599 1000

LVMH Tower [73]
19–21 East 57th Street
New York, NY 10022
T   212 931 2000
F   212 931 2099

Magnolia Bakery [48]
401 Bleecker Street
New York, NY 10014
T   212 462 2572

Marc Jacobs [172]
Menswear:
405 Bleecker Street
Marc:
403 Bleecker Street
New York, NY 10014

T   212 924 0026
W   www.marcjacobs.com

Mare Chiaro [158]
176 Mulberry Street
New York, NY 10013
T   212 226 9345

Matthew Marks Gallery [38]
523 West 24th Street
New York, NY 10011
T   212 243 0200
E   info@matthewmarks.com
W   www.matthewmarks.com

Maxilla and Mandible [87]
451 Columbus Avenue
New York, NY 10024
T   212 724 6173
W   www.maxillaand
    mandible.com

Max Protetch Gallery [41]
511 West 22nd Street
New York, NY 10011
T   212 633 6999
F   212 691 4342
E   info@maxprotetch.com
W   www.maxprotetch.com

Mayle [173]
252 Elizabeth Street
New York, NY 10012
T   212 625 0406

**McSorley's Old Ale
House** [151]
15 East 7th Street
New York, NY 10003
T   212 473 9148

McSweeney's Store [166]
429 Seventh Avenue
New York, NY 10001
T   718 499 9884
W   www.mcsweeneys.net

Me & Ro [169]
239 Elizabeth Street
New York, NY 10012
T   917 237 9215
F   917 237 9219
E   meandroretail@rcn.com
W   www.meandrojewelry.com

Meet [46]
71–73 Gansevoort Street
New York, NY 10014
T   212 242 0990
F   212 242 1952
E   info@the-meet.com
W   www.the-meet.com

Merc Bar [27]
151 Mercer Street
New York, NY 10012
T   212 966 2727
F   212 996 3329
W   www.mercbar.com

**Mercedes-Benz
Showroom** [73]
430 Park Avenue

New York, NY 10022
T   212 629 1666

**Merchant's House
Museum** [31]
29 East 4th Street
New York, NY 10003
T   212 777 1089
F   212 777 1104
E   nyc1832@
    merchantshouse.com
W   www.merchantshouse.com

**Metropolitan Museum
of Art** [84]
1000 Fifth Avenue
New York, NY 10028
T   212 535 7710
W   www.metmuseum.org

MoMA QNS [102]
4520 33rd Street
Long Island City, NY 11101
T   212 708 9400
E   info@moma.org
W   www.moma.org

Momenta Art [98]
72 Berry Street
Brooklyn, NY 11211
T   718 218 8058
W   www.momentaart.org

The Morgan Library [68]
29 East 36th Street
New York, NY 10016
T   212 685 0610
W   www.morganlibrary.org

Moss [167]
146 Greene Street
New York, NY 10012
T   212 204 7100
F   212 204 7101
E   customerservice@
    mossonline.com
W   www.mossonline.com

Moto [101]
394 Broadway
Brooklyn, NY 11211
T   718 599 6895
W   www.circa1938.com

**Municipal Art Society and
Urban Center Books** [72]
457 Madison Avenue
New York, NY 10022
T   212 935 3960
F   212 753 1816
E   info@mas.org
W   www.mas.org
Bookstore:
T   212 935 3592
F   212 223 2887
E   info@urbancenterbooks.org
W   www.urbancenterbooks.com

National Arts Club [55]
15 Gramercy Park South
New York, NY 10003
T   212 475 3424
W   www.nationalartsclub.org

Neue Galerie [87]
1048 Fifth Avenue
New York, NY 10028
T 212 628 6200
F 212 628 8824
E museum@neuegalerie.org
W www.neuegalerie.org

**New Museum of
Contemporary Art** [25]
583 Broadway
New York, NY 10012
T 212 219 1222
F 212 431 5328
E newmu@newmuseum.org
W www.newmuseum.org

**The New York
Earth Room** [28]
141 Wooster Street
New York, NY 10012
W www.diacenter.org

**New York Public
Library** [70]
Fifth Avenue and 42nd Street
New York, NY 10018
T 212 930 0830
W www.nypl.org

**New York Stock
Exchange** [62]
8 Broad Street
New York, NY 10005
T 212 56 5168
W www.nyse.com

Oak Bar [76]
The Plaza Hotel
768 Fifth Avenue
New York, NY 10019
T 212 546 5330

Odeon [141]
145 West Broadway
New York, NY 10013
T 212 233 0507

Other Music [31]
15 East 4th Street
New York, NY 10003
T 212 477 8150
W www.othermusic.com

Ouest [89]
2315 Broadway
New York, NY 10024
T 212 580 8700
F 212 580 1360
W www.ouestny.com

**Oyster Bar at Grand
Central** [141]
Grand Central Station
Lower Concourse
42nd Street
New York, NY 10017
T 212 490 6650
F 212 949 5210
E info@oysterbarny.com
W www.oysterbarny.com

Oznot's Dish [98]
79 Berry Street
Brooklyn, NY 11211
T 718 599 6596

Paley Park [69]
5 East 53rd Street
New York, NY 10022

The Park [152]
118 Tenth Avenue
New York, NY 10011
T 212 352 3313

Passerby [154]
436 West 15th Street
New York, NY 10011
T 212 206 7321

Pastis [46]
9 Ninth Avenue
New York, NY 10014
T 212 929 4844

Pearl River Mart [18]
477 Broadway
New York, NY 10013
T 212 431 4770
E info@pearlriver.com
W www.pearlriver.com

Peking Duck House [18]
28 Mott Street
New York, NY 10013
T 212 227 1810

Pete's Candy Store [97]
709 Lorimer Street
Brooklyn, NY 11211
T 718 302 3770
W www.petescandystore.com

**Peter Luger's
Steak House** [139]
178 Broadway
Brooklyn, NY 11211
T 718 387 7400
F 718 387 3523
E info@peterluger.com
W www.peterluger.com

Pete's Tavern [55]
129 East 18th Street
New York, NY 10003
T 212 473 7676
W www.petestavern.com

Pierogi 2000 [99]
177 North 9th Street
Brooklyn, NY 11211
T 718 599 2144
W www.pierogi2000.com

Prada [170]
575 Broadway
New York, NY 10012
T 212 334 8888

Printed Matter [40]
535 West 22nd Street
New York, NY 10011
T 212 925 0325

F 212 925 0464
W www.printedmatter.org

Prune [143]
54 East 1st Street
New York, NY 10003
T 212 677 6221

**P.S.1 Contemporary Art
Center** [102]
22–25 Jackson Avenue
Long Island City, NY 11101
T 718 784 2084
F 718 482 9454
E mail@ps1.org
W www.ps1.org

Rainbow Grill [76]
30 Rockefeller Plaza
65th Floor
New York, NY 10012
T 212 632 5100
F 212 632 5105
E reservations@cipriani.com
W www.cipriani.com/cipriani/
   RainbowGrill/grill.htm

Ralph Lauren [83]
867 Madison Avenue
New York, NY 10022
T 212 606 2100
W www.polo.com

The Red Cat [44]
227 Tenth Avenue
New York, NY 10011
T 212 242 1122
F 212 242 1390
W www.theredcat.com

Relish [101]
225 Wythe Avenue
Brooklyn, NY 11211
T 718 963 4546
W www.relish.com

**The Roosevelt Island
Tramway** [84]
59th Street and Second Avenue
W www.rioc.com

Russ & Daughters [58]
179 East Houston Street
New York, NY 10002
T 212 475 4880
F 212 475 0345
E info@russanddaughters.com
W www.russanddaughters.com

Russian Samovar [75]
256 West 52nd Street
New York, NY 10019
T 212 757 0168
F 212 765 2133
E info@russiansamovar.com
W www.russiansamovar.com

Screening Room [157]
54 Varick Street
New York, NY 10013
T 212 334 2100
F 212 334 8209
W www.thescreeningroom.com

Seize Sur Vingt [171]
243 Elizabeth Street
New York, NY 10012
T 212 343 0476
F 212 348 9589
E nyc@16sur20.com
W www.16sur20.com

Seven [60]
180 Orchard Street
New York NY 10002
T 646 654 0156

**Seventh Regiment
Armory** [84]
640 Park Avenue
New York, NY 10021

71 Clinton Fresh Food [60]
71 Clinton Street
New York, NY 10002
T 212 614 6960

**Sherwood Cafe at Robin
des Bois** [153]
195 Smith Street
Brooklyn, NY 11201
T 718 596 1609
W www.sherwoodcafe.com

Sigerson Morrison [164]
28 Prince Street
New York, NY 10012
T 212 219 3893
W www.sigersonmorrison.com

60 Thompson [118]
60 Thompson Street
New York, NY 10012
T 212 204 6465
F 212 431 0200
E info@60thompson.com
W www.60thompson.com

Skyscraper Museum [62]
39 Battery Place
New York, NY 100280
T 212 968 1961
W www.skyscraper.org

Smalls [48]
183 West 10th Street
New York, NY 10014
T 212 929 7565
W www.smallsjazz.com

**Socrates Sculpture
Park** [102]
Broadway at Vernon Boulevard
Long Island City, NY 11106
T 718 956 1819
F 718 626 1533
W www.socratessculpture
   park.org

**Solomon R. Guggenheim
Museum** [87]
1071 Fifth Avenue
New York, NY 10128
T 212 423 3500
W www.guggenheim.org

Spoonbill & Sugartown [101]
218 Bedford Avenue
Brooklyn, NY 11211
T   718 387 7322
E   info@spoonbillbooks.com
W   www.spoonbillbooks.com

Standard [57]
158 First Avenue
New York, NY 10009
T   212 387 0239
E   drink@standardbar.com
W   www.standardbar.com

**Starrett Lehigh
Building** [38]
601 West 26th Street
New York, NY 10001

Steinway & Sons [76]
109 West 57th Street
New York, NY 10019
T   212 246 1100
W   www.steinway.com

Steven Alan [165]
103 Franklin Street
New York, NY 10013
T   212 343 0692

Steven Salen Tailors [70]
18 East 53rd Street
New York, NY 10022
T   212 755 5665

**Storefront for Art
and Architecture** [18]
97 Kenmare Street
New York, NY 10012
T   212 431 5795
F   212 431 5755
E   info@storefrontnews.org
W   www.storefrontnews.org

**The Studio Museum
in Harlem** [90]
144 West 125th Street
New York, NY 10027
T   212 864 4500
F   212 864 4800
W   www.studiomuseum.org

Submercer [28]
Below Mercer Hotel
147 Mercer Street
New York, NY 10012
T   212 966 6060

Supreme [24]
274 Lafayette Street
New York, NY 10012
T   212 966 7799

**Sylvia's Soul Food
Restaurant** [90]
328 Lenox Avenue (Malcolm
X Boulevard)
New York, NY 10027
T   212 996 0660
F   212 427 6389
W   www.sylviassoulfood.com

Tabla [55]
11 Madison Avenue
New York, NY 10010
T   212 889 0667
F   212 889 0914

Takashimaya [76]
693 Fifth Avenue
New York, NY 10022
T   212 350 0100
F   212 350 0542
W   www.ny-takashimaya.com

Teany [150]
90 Rivington Street
New York, NY 10002
T   212 475 9190

Ted Muehling [22]
27 Howard Street
New York, NY 10013
T   212 431 3825
W   www.tedmuehling.com

Temple Bar [159]
332 Lafayette Street
New York, NY 10012
T   212 925 4242
W   www.templebarnyc.com

TG170 [60]
170 Ludlow Street
New York, NY 10002
T   212 995 8660
F   212 674 6972
E   terri@tg170.com
W   www.tg170.com

Théo [17]
325 Spring Street
New York, NY 10013
T   212 414 1344

Tiffany & Co. [72]
727 Fifth Avenue
New York, NY 10022
T   212 755 8000
W   www.tiffany.com

Totem [16]
71 Franklin Street
T   212 925 5506
F   212 925 5082
83 Grand Street
T   212 219 2446
F   212 219 2780
New York, NY 10013
E   info@totemdesign.com
W   www.totemdesign.com

Town [142]
Chambers Hotel
15 West 56th Street
New York, NY 10019
T   212 582 4445
W   www.townnyc.com

Tribeca Grand Hotel [132]
2 Sixth Avenue
New York, NY 10013
T   212 519 6677
W   www.tribecagrand.com

Tribeca Issey Miyake [17]
119 Hudson Street
New York, NY 10013
T   212 226 0100
F   212 428 6758
W   www.isseymiyake.com

Unis [21]
226 Elizabeth Street
New York, NY 10012
T   212 431 5533

**United Nations
Headquarters** [70]
First Avenue at 46th Street
New York, NY 10017
T   212 963 8687
E   inquiries@un.org
W   www.un.org/tours

Ursus Rare Books [84]
Mezzanine of Carlyle Hotel
981 Madison Avenue
New York, NY 10021
T   212 772 8787
F   212 737 9306
W   www.ursusbooks.com

Vesuvio Bakery [28]
160 Prince Street
New York, NY 10012
T   212 925 8248

Visionaire [22]
11 Mercer Street
New York, NY 10013
T   212 274 8959
F   212 343 2596
W   www.visionaireworld.com

Vitra Showroom [43]
29 Ninth Avenue
New York, NY 10014
T   212 929 3626
F   212 929 6424
W   www.vitra.com

WD-50 [60]
50 Clinton Street
New York, NY 10002
T   212 477 2900

Wild Lily Tearoom [43]
511–A West 22nd Street
New York, NY 10011
T   212 691 2258
F   212 691 7985
W   www.wildlilytearoom.com

Zabar's [88]
2245 Broadway
New York, NY 10024
T   212 787 2000
F   212 580 4477
E   info@zabars.com
W   www.zabars.com

Ziegfeld Theater [76]
141 West 54th Street
New York, NY 10019
T   212 765 7601
W   www.clearviewcinemas.com

CATSKILLS [178]

*Saugerties does not have a train
,station, but from Penn Station you
can take the Amtrak rail line to
Rhinecliff (15 miles [24 kilometers]
to the east of Saugerties) or from
Grand Central Station the
MetroNorth commuter service to
Poughkeepsie, then get a taxi to
Saugerties. By car, the drive takes
an hour and forty-five minutes up
the west side of the Hudson River
along the Palisades Parkway and
then the New York State Thruway
North (I-87). The Villa at Saugerties
is a couple of miles outside the
town. For detailed directions use
their website.*

Storm King Art Center
Old Pleasant Hill Road
Mountainville, NY 10953
T   845 534 3115
W   www.stormkingartcenter.org
*Open April–December,
Wednesday–Sunday*

Café Tamayo
89 Partition Street
Saugerties, NY 12477
T   845 246 9371
E   tamayo@ulster.net
W   www.cafetamayo.com

The Villa at Saugerties
159 Fawn Road
Saugerties, NY 12477
T   845 246 0682
E   upstatevilla@aol.com
W   www.thevillaatsaugerties.com
Double rooms from $140

BUCKS COUNTY [180]
*If you are not driving, take the bus
from Port Authority bus station,
Manhattan, to Frenchtown,
Pennsylvania. Take a taxi one mile
(1.6 kilometers) to the EverMay on
the Delaware in the village of
Erwinna. Bus schedules can be
found at www.transbridgebus.com/
sched_frenchny.htm*

EverMay on the Delaware
River Road, Erwinna
Bucks County, PA 18920
T   610 294 9100
E   info@evermay.com
W   www.evermay.com
Double rooms from $160

Fonthill
East Court Street and Swap Road
(Route 313)
Doylestown, PA 18901
T   215 348 9461
W   www.mercermuseum.org/
     fonthill

The Mercer Museum
84 South Pine Street.
Doylestown, PA 18901
T   215 230 0823
W   www.mercermuseum.org/
     mercermuseum

Golden Nugget Antique Flea
Market
1850 River Road
Lambertville, NJ 08530
T   609 397 0811
E   info@gnmarket.com
W   www.gnmarket.com

Lambertville Antique Flea Market
1864 River Road
Route 29 (one mile south [1.6
kilometers] of Lambertsville)
Lambertville, NJ 08530
T   609 397 0456

HUDSON RIVER VALLEY [182]
Take the MetroNorth rail service
from Grand Central Station to
Beacon and then take it one stop
back towards New York to Cold
Spring. By car, take Palisades
Parkway North, cross Bear
Mountain Bridge and take Route
90 north to Beacon. The journey is
approximately 90 minutes.

Dia: Beacon
3 Beekman Street
Beacon, NY 12508
T   212 989 5566
E   info@diabeacon.org
W   www.diabeacon.org

Pig Hill Inn
73 Main Street
Cold Spring, NY 10516
T   845 265 9247
E   pighillinn@aol.com
W   www.pighillinn.com
Double rooms from $145

East Side Kitchen
124 Main Street
Cold Spring, NY 10516
T   845 265 7223
W   www.eastsidekitchen.com

EAST HAMPTON [184]
*By car, take the I-27 along the
south fork of Long Island to
Bridgehampton and East Hampton.
For Shelter Island, take the ferry
from Sag Harbor. The train journey
from Penn Station to East Hampton
on the LIRR takes about two and a
half hours: further information is
available by calling 718 217 5477.
You can also take the Hampton
Jitney bus: information and details
on 631 283 4600 or 800 936 0440.*

Glen Horowitz Bookseller
87 Newtown Lane
East Hampton, NY 11937
T   631 324 5511

Pollock-Krasner House
830 Fireplace Road
East Hampton, NY 11937
T   631 324 4929
W   naples.cc.sunysb.edu/
     CAS/pkhouse.nsf

The Dan Flavin Art Institute
Corwith Avenue off Main Street
Bridgehampton, NY 11932
T 631 324 1476
W   www.diacenter.org/ltproj/
     flavbrid
Open May through September

Sunset Beach Hotel
35 Shore Road
Shelter Island, NY 11965
T   631 749 2001
F   631 749 1843
Double rooms from $245

1770 House
143 Main Street
East Hampton, NY 11937
T   631 324 1770
W   www.1770house.com
Double rooms from $250